THE AUDUBON SOCIETY

by Les Line, Editor of Audubon magazine, and Lorus and Margery Milne

A Chanticleer Press Edition

BOOK OF INSECTS

HARRY N. ABRAMS, INC., PUBLISHERS, NEW YORK

Library of Congress Cataloging in Publication Data
Line, Les.
The Audubon Society book of insects.
"A Chanticleer Press edition."
Includes index.
   1. Insects.   I. Milne, Lorus Johnson, 1912–
II. Milne, Margery Joan Greene, 1914–
III. National Audubon Society.   IV. Title.
QL463.L44   1983   595.7   82-16457
ISBN 0-8109-1806-4
Published in 1983 by Harry N. Abrams, Incorporated, New York

Trademark "Audubon Society" used by publisher under license by the
National Audubon Society, Inc.

Prepared and produced by Chanticleer Press, Inc.
Manufactured in Japan

Chanticleer Staff:
Publisher: Paul Steiner
Editor-in-Chief: Gudrun Buettner
Managing Editor: Susan Costello
Project Editor: Ann Whitman
Natural Science Editor: John Farrand, Jr.
Assistant Editor: Jonathan P. Roth
Production: Helga Lose, John Holliday
Art Director: Carol Nehring
Picture Library: Joan Lynch, Edward Douglas
Design: Massimo Vignelli

First four frontispieces: *Leaf-cutter ants* (Atta *sp.*) *systematically
remove petals from a sunflower in Panama.* (Raymond A. Mendez)

Fifth frontispiece: *Beetle tracks at dawn on a sand dune in Utah.*
(Betty Randall)

*Notes on Illustration Numbers: All illustrations are numbered
according to the pages on which they appear.*

Contents

Preface

The paper wasps are busy in the upper corner of my study window as I sit at the typewriter. Having found a narrow gap between the frame and storm window, a team of female wasps last spring built a sturdy apartment house of a fast-hardening mass of wood pulp and saliva. I count about 180 hexagonal cells in the uncovered, single-tiered comb; perhaps a third are presently sealed as larvae pupate into the next generation of workers.

My daughter was painfully stung at an early age by a yellow jacket; now she shrieks whenever a paper wasp finds its way into the house. She remains unconvinced by my assurances that wasps of the genus *Polistes* are mild-mannered and quite tolerant of humans. She does not understand why I haven't zapped the comb with wasp-killing spray, preferring instead to watch the progress of the colony as autumn approaches.

I do, however, have a healthy respect for the hornets whose huge globular nest hangs in an ash tree at the edge of my woods. I remember the summer day, long ago, when a boyhood chum threw a baseball at such a nest. Need I say that the ball game was abruptly cancelled?

Beyond the study window, squadrons of Japanese beetles swarm about three small cherry trees whose foliage has been thoroughly riddled. Although it is chiefly known as a destructive pest, attacking more than 200 plants ranging from sweet corn to fruit trees, this beetle is still admired for its beauty: the half-inch oval body of *Popilla japonica* is a bright metallic green, accented by reddish-orange elytra.

Japanese beetle larvae were accidentally carried to

North America in 1916 with the roots of imported iris, and the species soon became a major villain. I know it well. My first big conservation battle, as a spokesman for the Michigan Audubon Society, was a crusade to prevent state agriculture officials from raining dieldrin, one of the most toxic pesticides known, across farmlands and suburbs to halt the insect's spread. What the poison purveyors promised was the beetle's "eradication." What they delivered instead was a wildlife holocaust.

Insects—we tend to ignore them until they compel us to sit up and take notice. Until they become a minor irritation—the ants in the kitchen, the hornworms on the tomatoes, the aphids on the roses. Or until they become a real or imagined problem—threatening our health, our crops, our treasured shade trees. (Yes, a good many insect "problems" are concocted out of thin air for the purpose of selling chemical pesticides.)

I've been as guilty as most people of overlooking— avoiding?—the wonderful world of insects. What opened my eyes was an assignment to take photographs for a children's book on milkweed. I soon discovered a vast insect community closely linked to this common wildflower of field and roadside—not only butterflies, especially the famous monarch whose very survival depends on milkweed, but moths large and small, diurnal and nocturnal; longhorn beetles and ladybird beetles; bees and wasps; aphids and aphid-tending ants.

Thus I welcomed Paul Steiner's suggestion that we add to this marvelous series of Audubon Society Books a spectacular volume on insects and spiders. This book is

fully the equal of its predecessors, classics that
celebrate the worlds of birds, mammals, marine
wildlife, wildflowers, and trees.

It is nearly dusk now, and the night chorus has begun
in the woods and fields beyond my open study window.
I pause and listen with appreciation to the voices of
crickets, cicadas, and, most distinctive of all, the
katydids. Edwin Way Teale, a great naturalist of our
day who was fascinated all his life by the insect world,
called this chorus a "storm of contention that fills the
summer nights." He wrote of how the insect music
slows as autumn wanes, as nights become cooler. Of
how the crisp "Katy-did, Katy-didn't" of August
becomes a whispered, abbreviated "she-did" in late
October as the players lose the energy to vigorously
scrape their wings, their bows, together. "Although
they show no awareness of it, the end of their whole
generation is close at hand. Painfully slow now among
the remaining leaves, the musicians play on. Each year
at this time I am profoundly moved by this unconscious
lament, a lingering, sad farewell by those who do not
know they are going."

So, too, will the wasps in the corner of my window go
as winter approaches. The entire colony will perish
except for a handful of mated young queens. They will
overwinter in leaf litter in the nearby woods; come
spring, perhaps in the opposite corner of my window in
another narrow gap, they will begin to build a new
comb for the new year's first generation. I will
welcome them.

Les Line

Foreword

At the lawn's edge near the old house in Connecticut stood a tall "butterfly bush"—a Buddleia. Each year, from July until October, it produced an abundance of pale lavender flowers on long, slender spikes. During the barefoot days of summer, whenever no other exciting adventure could be dreamed up, I could always go out to the "butterfly bush," never knowing what strange new visitor I might find, balancing itself with fluttering wings on the tiny blossoms, and probing for the sweet nectar within. Since these flowers were rich in nectar, they attracted a seemingly endless succession of butterflies—handsome Black Swallowtails, boldly patterned Tiger Swallowtails, orange-and-black Monarchs, Mourning Cloaks that seemed clad in dark velvet, Great Spangled Fritillaries, Red Admirals, Painted Ladies, Cabbage Whites, a number of different sulphurs, and a host of tiny skippers, blues, and hairstreaks. The Buddleia towered over me, and these strange and shy creatures seemed to have come from another world, into which they quickly disappeared if I failed to approach them slowly and carefully.

It wasn't long before I began to follow the butterflies beyond the edge of the lawn and into the meadow and the patch of woods with its shallow, tumbling stream. Here I found vast numbers of other insects and spiders, less conspicuous, but no less interesting. Through the dense jungle of grass moved hordes of ants, which lived in colonies that reminded me of small human settlements in a trackless forest, and crickets that sang persistently in the summer heat. Tiny green leafhoppers flitted away in front of me as

I advanced through the grass, and fleet-footed wolf spiders often galloped across my hand or arm as I sat in the meadow gazing in wonder at the life it contained. In the woods, I found delicately patterned moths, almost invisible as they clung to the rough bark of the trees; great carabid beetles that darted through the leaf litter in pursuit of their prey; dragonflies that coasted through the air above the stream on rustling wings; and slow-moving, green katydids that were hard to find during the day, but whose nocturnal chorus of mating calls was as much a part of late summer, and as much of a warning that school days were approaching, as the appearance of asters and goldenrod, the gradually changing colors of the trees, and the dull-colored warblers that were migrating southward.

While these backyard insects are numerous and varied enough to occupy one's attention for a lifetime, I discovered much later that they are only a pale reflection of the abundant and bizarre insect life of the tropics. In South America I saw great *Morpho* butterflies, huge creatures with brilliant blue, mirrorlike wings; a giant ant the Indians call *isango*, whose sting is powerful enough to send you to the hospital for a week; lanternflies, distant cousins of the leafhoppers from back home, that glow in the dark; praying mantids, delicately pink, that mimic the flowers as they wait among them for their prey; and huge tarantulas or "bird spiders," some of them dangerous to man. In Africa, there were termites that build rock-hard mounds many feet tall, designed to provide a natural form of air conditioning; a butterfly whose mimicry is so highly developed that this single species can resemble a dozen or more other butterflies, each one toxic and avoided by predators; and swarms of migratory locusts that can devastate a farmer's crop in a single day.

Although from the human point of view insects are small—the smallest is a tiny wasp only two-tenths of a millimeter long, ironically named *Alaptus magnanimus*—they are far more numerous and adaptable than any other land-dwelling animals. More than a million species have been described by scientists, and several million more no doubt await discovery. They have established themselves in every habitat from snowfields high in the Himalayas to tide pools, from deep tropical rain forests to the turbulent surface of the ocean. The only habitat they have never successfully invaded is the world beneath the surface of the sea, and that is probably because their relatives the crustaceans got there first. So adaptable are the insects that for almost every organic substance found on earth, there is an insect that feeds on it. Some eat plant matter—leaves, flowers, wood, seeds, roots, and bark. Others are predators, hunting down other insects, tiny soil organisms, and even small mammals and birds. Insects feed on dung, pollen, algae, carrion, blood, and minute fragments of decaying leaves. In turn, they are preyed upon by animals of every kind and even by plants such as sundews, bladderwort, Venus' flytrap, and pitcher plants. As predators and prey, they are an integral part of every ecosystem in which they occur.

Because of their immense and varied ways of life, it is inevitable that they have come into competition with man. Every crop plant has its insect pests; every kind of livestock has insects that plague it. They are the vectors of many diseases, and they attack stored foodstuffs as readily as growing ones. Dealing with this competition is a challenge that man has yet to master. The widespread use of pesticides has created problems as great as those these chemicals were intended to solve, and the control of our insect competitors is being carried out in an increasingly cautious and biologically sound way, by enlisting the unwitting support of the insects' own enemies—their predators and parasites—and by skillfully manipulating the crop plants. But it is a battle that will probably never end.

Insects have their positive side as well. One species, the Honeybee, is responsible for pollinating dozens of crop species. Most wild plants are pollinated by insects. Easily raised in the laboratory, insects have been used in experiments that have taught us much, not only about the biology of the insects themselves, but about basic processes of life. This new knowledge has been used in a variety of ways to benefit mankind —in health, agriculture, and the intelligent use of our natural resources.

Insects provide another benefit that is impossible to measure or to put a price tag on. In their great abundance and diversity, they are fellow inhabitants of our fragile planet Earth. However different from us they may seem, they are the descendants and products of the same evolutionary forces that have shaped our own species. They must face and solve the same problems of survival that we face. From the most conspicuous and beautiful butterflies that have captivated children the world over, to parasitic wasps so tiny that they can rear their young from the nutrients contained in a single egg of another insect species, their varied ways of life are a source of wonder and delight. The more we know of them, and the more closely we peer into their secret world, the greater this sense of wonder becomes.

This splendid volume, the sixth in a series sponsored by the National Audubon Society, enables us to take this closer look, both at the insects and spiders that live close to home and at the remarkable insects of tropical lands. My friends Lorus and Margery Milne have written an admirable collection of essays that make the insects they write about appear larger than life, and that help us to share their fascination with these creatures they have studied for so many years. The superb photographs, enhanced by Les Line's informative and perceptive captions, give us an unequalled view of the inhabitants of the world of the insects. Paul Steiner and Chanticleer Press have produced a book that is as engaging an invitation to enjoy the insects and their world as a "butterfly bush" was to a small boy in Connecticut many years ago.

John Farrand, Jr.

For Joseph and Mary McDaniel, with gratitude.

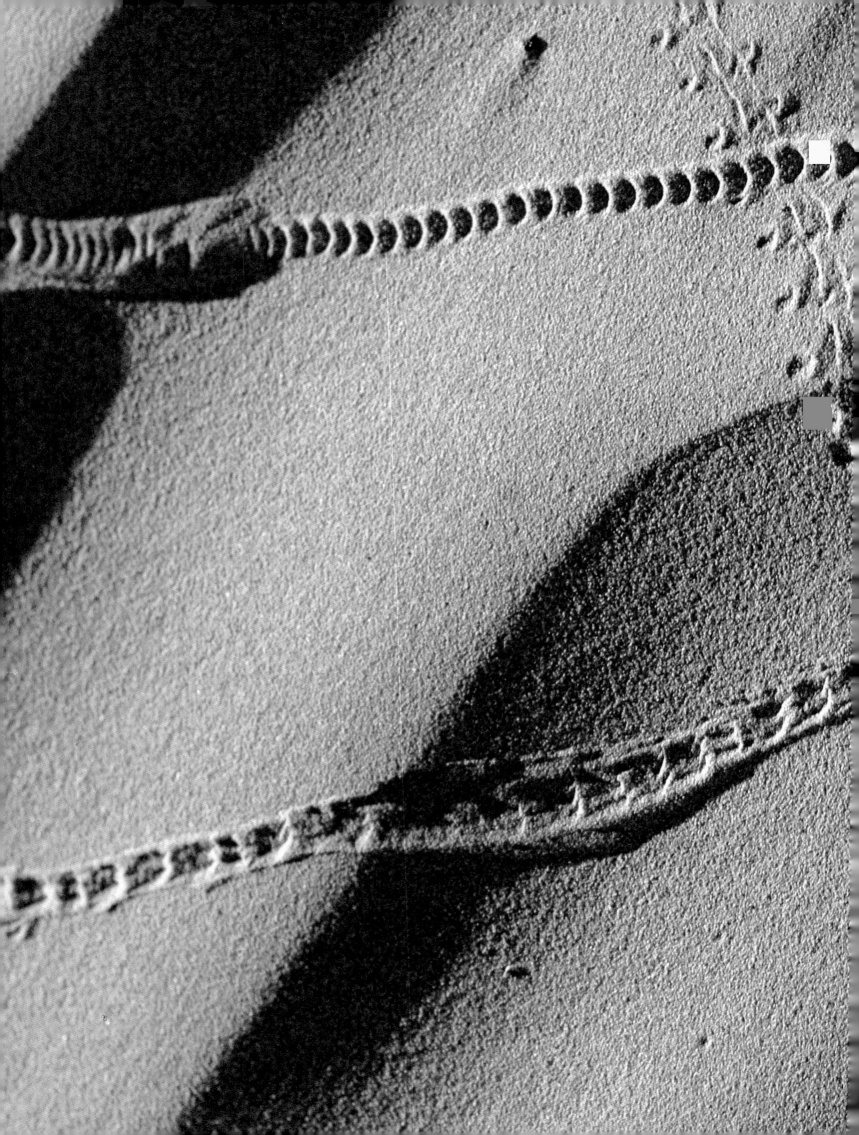

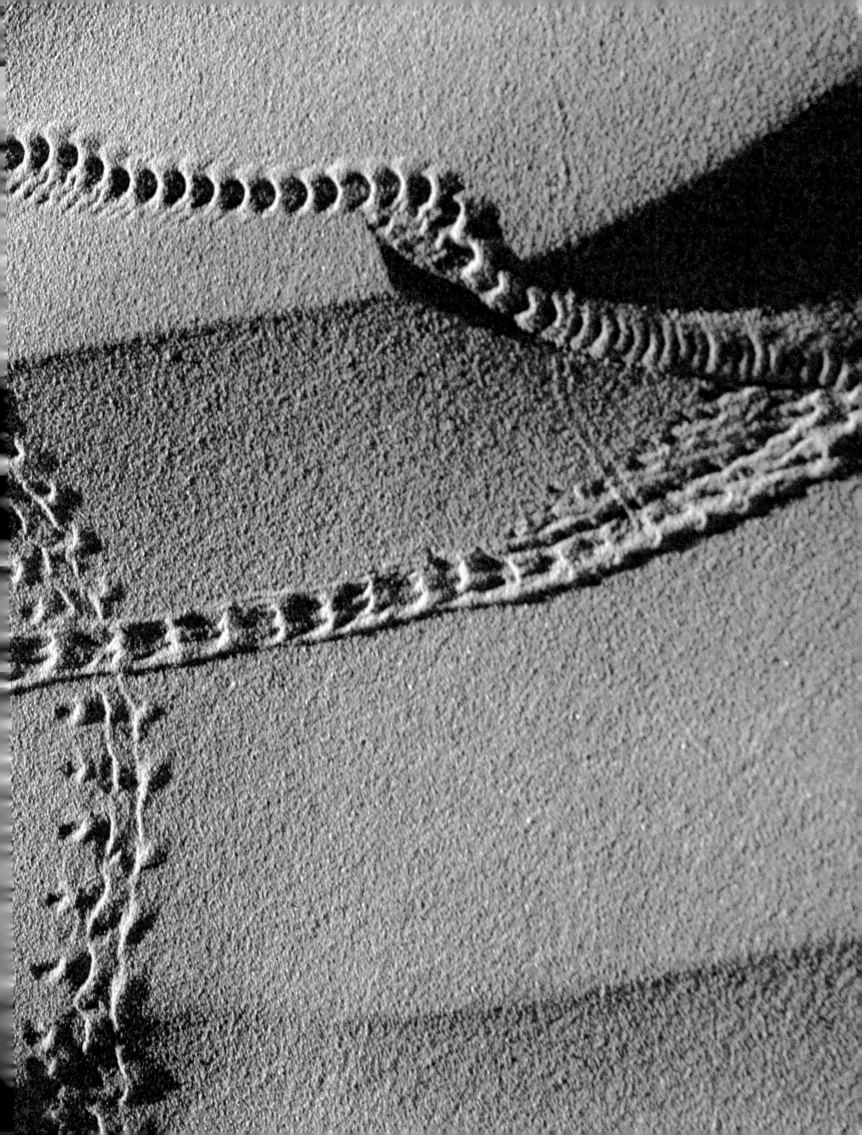

16. *A lined June beetle (Polyphylla sp.) scurries over a coral-tinted sand dune in southern Utah, leaving sharp evidence of its passing. An inch or more long, the big June beetles are noted for the long and broad plates that form the male's antennal clubs. June beetles lay their eggs near the base of woody plants; the larvae work their way into the soil, feeding on the roots. On warm summer evenings, June beetles gather around artificial lights; if picked up and held, they will squeak in protest.* (Betty Randall)

Bombardiers and Borers

Beetles have the right to claim a position as the most important and successful animals on earth. With about 300,000 different kinds alive today, and some 30,000 species in North America alone, the members of this order outnumber not only all other insects but the rest of the animal kingdom as well. Anyone who attempts to become familiar with all the beetles in the world has a challenging future. Wherever an insect of any kind can live, several kinds of beetles are at home. Some beetle species burrow in the soil or in the wood of trees; many feed on roots or foliage, or scavenge the remains of dead animals; and still others prey upon weaker insects or small fishes and tadpoles in fresh water.

The secret of this outstanding success seems to be the near indestructibility of most beetles. The head and body are protected by armorlike plates, and even the first pair of wings (called elytra) is part of this armor. In flight, the elytra are held stiffly aside while the membranous second pair of wings, usually longer than the elytra, provides propulsion. At rest, the second pair is folded near the tips and is shielded by the first pair, which closes together over the back, generally meeting along the midline.

In the air, beetles progress at moderate speed and maneuver rather poorly. A flying beetle that meets with an obstacle simply folds its wings and proceeds along the ground on its six sturdy legs. If the obstacle is the bark of a tree or a branch with edible leaves, the beetle may use its strong jaws instead, cutting a passageway or eating fragments of the foliage. Male stag beetles of the family Lucanidae use their oversize jaws in combat; two or more may battle for the right to mate with a nearby female. Many beetles use their jaws effectively as pinching organs in self-defense.

The most active beetles are often the most brilliantly colored. Shiny green tiger beetles (Cicindelidae) skitter like jewels along woodland paths. As you approach a watchful tiger beetle, it flies ahead rapidly for a few yards, then alights, turning quickly to face you, ready for its next move in this little game. The humpbacked tiger beetle larva lives in a pit and waits in ambush there, ready to reach out and capture an ant or other small prey that comes close to it.

Equally brilliant in green or bronze are the metallic wood borers (Buprestidae). The females excavate pits as egg sites in the bark of appropriate trees; upon hatching, the larva digs more deeply into the wood and feeds on it. Adults often rest on the bark of a tree, reflecting the sunlight from their bodies. If approached, the metallic borer leaps into flight and finds a new resting place.

In most parts of the world, when a stone is lifted or a log rolled aside, one or more ground beetles (Carabidae) are likely to run for cover. Deprived of shelter and exposed to the unwelcome combination of daylight and dry air, the insects hurry away or find new seclusion by thrusting their heads deep into some small, dark hole.

Certain ground beetles have strong defenses. Barely more than a quarter-inch long, with powder-blue wing covers and pale brownish-orange bodies, the bombardier beetles (*Brachinus* spp.) are aptly named: when alarmed, these insects discharge a little puff of brown gas, like smoke. The explosive popping sound accompanying this display is the result of the combination of the chemical substances from two separate glands. One releases a solution that is 25 percent hydrogen peroxide and 10 percent hydroquinone. The other provides enzymes which facilitate the instantaneous explosion. The combined chemical substances reach the temperature of boiling water, providing enough heat to vaporize fully a fifth of the fluid. The discharge consists of a hot jet of steam and minute droplets of quinone, which can discourage an attacking ant or, if repeated close to human fingers, stain the skin dark brown as though with iodine and confer a distinctive odor.

Four or five little explosions in quick succession usually empty the insect's defensive apparatus. Just occasionally we meet a bombardier beetle with a "six-shooter." Thomas Eisner of Cornell University discovered one exceptional bombardier, who responded to continued stimulation with twenty-nine shots before giving up. All bombardiers earn high scores for marksmanship, making direct hits in almost any direction by turning the flexible nozzle of the defensive organ.

As a general rule, the more brilliant and conspicuous beetles will less often try to escape approach. Brilliant, conspicuous beetles tend to have a defense system, often chemical in nature, that makes them dangerous or unpalatable to any creature that jostles or swallows them. One whole family, that of the oil beetles (Meloidae), shows this characteristic. Its members rest on flowers or foliage, unwilling to move and without concern for being seen. Each of them secretes within its body a potent substance called cantharidin, which is so toxic that a tiny drop of it on human skin will produce a painful blister. Some of these beetles exude droplets of the secretion from their knee joints when disturbed. Others store the material in minute pockets within their wing covers, where it is likely to affect only an animal that eats the beetle.

Even the seemingly harmless ladybug beetle (Coccinellidae) exudes a yellowish liquid when disturbed, as though the odor (and perhaps the taste) of this fluid would repel an attacker. The beetle runs about in plain sight, where its almost hemispherical shape, reddish-orange color, and black markings can be seen at close range. The best place to find these beetles is on the surface of a plant that is infested with aphids and scale insects. These sap-sucking insects are devoured in great numbers by both the adult ladybug beetle and its black larvae, thereby reducing the damage done to the host plant through loss of sap. The benefits brought by ladybugs were well known to the grape-growers of medieval Europe, who dedicated the beetle to the Virgin Mary as the "Beetle of Our Lady."

The well-known nursery rhyme that urges the ladybug to ". . . fly away home/Your house is on fire, and your children do roam" arose from the widespread European practice of burning vines after the grape harvest. A second verse, less widely known, continues, "Except little Nan, who sits in a pan/Weaving gold laces as fast as she can." "Nan" was the pupating larva, which produces a little mat of golden silk on a leaf, with hardening strands of saliva. The larva attaches its body to the mat and remains there throughout its transformation to adult. Ladybug beetles of all ages—adults, larvae, and pupae—must be unpalatable to insect-eaters, since they rarely conceal themselves and are conspicuously marked. Hundreds of these little beetles seek out sheltered places in which to survive together the cold of winter, clinging under bark or to the sides of large boulders, out of the wind. Their numbers may indicate merely that these places are exactly the shelter each beetle needs. It is equally possible that the odor of many ladybugs clustered together discourages the insect-eaters more effectively than would the odor of a single hibernating beetle. We find these impressive aggregations all across the northern states, in adjacent Canada, and at higher elevations in California.

Fireflies (Lampyridae) are true beetles with the uncanny ability to produce light without heat by means of a chemical called luciferin. They use their luminous organs to send coded messages in darkness, all in the interest of reproduction. The male flies back and forth above a meadow, using his large compound eyes to scan the surrounding landscape. He flashes a message to indicate his interest in a mate. Seeing it, a female of his kind responds with her light. The male makes a quick U-turn and flashes again, and the female replies. He comes in for a landing on the leaf where she rests. There the two insects confirm their compatibility with chemical signals and proceed to mate.

So open a communication system is vulnerable to fraud. Recently, some female fireflies were found to signal to males of species other than their own, then to devour the unsuspecting suitor that arrived. After such a meal, the female may attract a proper mate and have her eggs fertilized for laying. The eggs of some fireflies are luminous, but it is not known what purpose the luminosity serves. The black larvae, which hunt for smaller insects as prey among leaf litter on the ground, often have luminous spots that make them visible in darkness; they may be mistaken for glowworms. True glowworms, however, are adults, either of wingless luminous females of certain

European fireflies or the equally luminous females of a North American beetle in the genus *Phengodes* of a related family, the Phengodidae.

Fire beetles are luminous members of the family of click beetles (Elateridae). Fire beetles live in tropical America as well as Florida and Texas. Panamanian ladies regard these beetles as spectacular ornaments for evening garb, and sometimes wear these *cucujos* like brooches immobilized by wire harnesses. During the construction of the Panama Canal, a surgical operation was continued one night, despite a power failure, by the light from a jar of *cucujos*.

With or without luminous spots, a click beetle has a special way of freeing itself if captured, or of turning itself right side up if it tumbles on its back. The flexible joint between the thorax and the abdomen is equipped on the underside with a projecting fingerlike process and a matching socket. The insect slips the process out of the socket and tenses the muscles of its body, then lets the process slip back into the socket. The whole body snaps into a new position. The jerking action may flip the beetle out of a captor's grip or toss it into the air from an upside-down position, leaving to chance whether the body will land feet downward and allow the beetle to make its escape.

Click beetles come in many sizes, some over three inches long. The Eyed Click Beetle (*Alaus oculatus*) of eastern North America is an impressive denizen of deciduous and mixed woods that contain an abundance of rotting logs; this species may be 1¾ inches long. The adult appears to eat little, but the hungry larva is a hard-surfaced "wireworm" that feeds on many kinds of roots and also preys on soft-bodied animals of woodland soil. The dull, dark brown click beetles, with their slender bodies just one-third of an inch long, are much more numerous but can be easily overlooked.

Forests and fields with woody shrubs provide many opportunities for beetles with extraordinarily elongated antennae (Cerambycidae), known popularly as "longicorns." The antennae of males of the Black Pine Sawyer (*Monochamus scutellatus*) of eastern North America often reach two inches, twice the length of the body. The name "Sawyer" for this longicorn refers to the sound the larva creates as it gnaws deep tunnels, feeding on the firm wood of pine trees. These actions set the whole tree vibrating as though a saw were in use. Adult longicorns of many kinds rest inconspicuously on tree bark. Others, often more brightly colored, visit flowers for pollen and nectar. All are quick to fly if approached, probably because of their good vision rather than any sensory action of their antennae.

Quite different antennae earn the scarab beetles (Scarabaeidae) the name "lamellicorns." The clublike tips of the antennae can be fanned open to expose a series of parallel plates (lamellae), on the surface of which are the sense organs for smell. The name provides a useful grouping because this family includes beetles with many different ways of life. Many are dung beetles, which scavenge and rear their grublike larvae in animal wastes. They recycle these materials and make them available as nutrients for plants. The most famous beetle to engage in this practice is the Sacred Scarab (*Scarabaeus sacer*) of Mediterranean countries, which works dung into a ball and then rolls it over the ground to a place where the soil is soft. There the beetle digs out the earth, letting the ball sink below the surface where it will not be taken by any other creature. A scarab egg is laid on the ball; when it hatches, the larva feeds to full size. Ancient Egyptians identified this beetle with their sun god Ra, who rolled the sun across the sky from dawn to dusk; they also found symbolism in the five joints of each of the six feet—a total of thirty, like the days of the month. Roman legionnaires adopted the Sacred Scarab for their banners, and the respect accorded this dung beetle continued. Related scarabs show a further development in behavior: the male and female of a pair cooperate in rolling the ball and sinking it into the earth.

The famous Japanese Beetle (*Popillia japonica*), which gained entry into the United States in 1916 and spread widely despite efforts to control it, is now found from Maine to Florida and attacks more than 200 different plants, with disastrous consequences. May beetles, also known as "June bugs," are members of the genus *Phyllophaga;* these are the familiar beetles that fly onto the screens of lighted windows and buzz noisily. As adults, May beetles also eat some foliage. Their C-shaped white larvae feed in soil on roots of herbs, shrubs, and trees, but seldom do as much damage as those of the Japanese Beetle in similar situations.

Tropical scarabs come in gigantic sizes and grotesque forms. The biggest is the Goliath Beetle (*Goliathus giganteus*) of the Congo rainforests, which can grow to six inches long and weigh as much as a rat. There, one July day, we had our interpreter ask members of a nomadic group of Ituri Pygmies if they could catch one for us. The spokesman for the group explained that the season was wrong. He talked and talked, gesturing enthusiastically and drawing horizontal circles in the air with his forefinger. Translated, his story told of Pygmy youngsters tying the giant insects to the end of a stick with flexible fibers from a plant. The beetles would fly in circles, buzzing without getting anywhere; eventually, the Pygmy insisted, the children always released their living toys. The beetle itself is too heavily armored to be edible, but it does lay eggs in rotting wood. There the Pygmies dig at the proper time of year to reach the enormous C-shaped grubs that, to an acquired taste, are delicious either raw or lightly roasted over the campfire.

Quite different and half the size of the Goliath Beetle are the rhinoceros beetles of tropical America, named for the long projections from body and head. One specimen we discovered in a Panamanian rainforest was four inches long, almost two inches wide, and more than an inch thick. Pressing thumb and fingers against opposite sides of the beetle, we picked it up, only to have it raise its legs and shove our fingers aside. The only secure hold we could find was on its head horn. Gripped otherwise, the beetle freed itself in just a few seconds.

Interaction between the sexes is quite extensive among the burying beetles (*Nicrophorus* spp., Silphidae). These one-inch-long black insects with bright orange stripes across their wing covers are specialists. The adults seem remarkable enough when they crawl, inverted, under a dead mouse, sparrow, or snake on hard ground, then lift it, transporting the prize to a softer spot as much as fifteen feet away. There the beetle, or a pair of them, digs out the earth, secreting the body in the ground for future food for itself and its family. After the body is concealed, usually before daybreak, it is worked into a spherical form within the burial chamber, eaten, then regurgitated as partly digested meat for the young that hatch from eggs laid in an adjacent tunnel. Young and adults of both sexes communicate by scratching sounds. Both parents generally stay in attendance until the larvae are ready to pupate. Rarely among cold-blooded animals is a male so attentive and cooperative with his mate or even so aware of his young.

Far more casual mating antics are shown by the heavily armored weevil (Curculionidae), whose head is prolonged forward into a beak with the jaws at the tip. Large species are often called snout beetles or billbugs. All members of this family feed on plants. Females use their beaks and jaws to bore into stems, fruits, or seeds and lay an egg in each hole. The C-shaped grubs that hatch there are frequently destructive. A few species have been used to control unwanted weed plants, but other weevils detract from the benefits obtained from these few. The infamous Boll Weevil (*Anthonomus grandis*), originally from Mexico and a mere quarter of an inch long, destroys much of the cotton bolls on the crop plant; the larva, hidden inside the boll, is almost unreachable by control measures.

Foliage as exclusive food has become the specialty of more than 20,000 species of beetles in a family of "leaf beetles" (Chrysomelidae). One kind that spread from the New World to the Old, attacking potato plants, is the Colorado Potato Beetle (*Leptinotarsa decimlineata*). As though in exchange, America got from Europe the Elm-leaf Beetle (*Galerucella luteola*), the unwanted asparagus beetles (*Crioceris asparagi* and *C. duodecimpunctata*)—both of which habitually attack cucumbers as well—together with a number of other kinds.

Even the most pesky beetles are handsome when viewed at close range, revealing a beautiful symmetry of markings and pits in their amazing armor. With their hard outer coverings and ability to survive while getting about, they succeed in a multitude of ways, producing generous families. Beetles will undoubtedly be our companions on Earth as long as humankind exists.

25. *Weather has peeled the bark from a dead birch tree in northern Germany, uncovering the mines of larvae of the Birch Bark Beetle (Scolytus ratzeburgi). Adult bark or engraver beetles—a quarter-inch or less in size—deposit their eggs in the inner bark of a host tree, each species of beetle attacking a certain kind of tree. Feeding on the inner bark, the larvae bore away from the central brood gallery, creating a complex pattern of tunnels that is characteristic of their particular species. If their tunnels girdle the cambium layer, the tree will die. Bark beetles can cause serious economic damage, especially in coniferous forests. And the European Elm Bark Beetle (Scolytus multistriatus), accidentally introduced into North America, carries a fungus which has devastated the stately American elm across the continent. (Heiko Bellmann/Bildarchiv Jürgen Lindenburger)*

26. *Pressed tightly against a leaf in the Costa Rican forest, a tortoise beetle (subfamily Cassidinae) becomes a difficult tidbit for a predator to pick up. With its head hidden beneath an oval, deeply sculpted body, a tortoise beetle does indeed suggest a tiny turtle. In the tropics, tortoise beetles often are large and brightly colored; some species are used in jewelry, although the metallic hues usually fade after the insect's death.* (Carroll W. Perkins)

27 *top. A male giraffe weevil* (Paratrachelophorus sp.) *from Laos really isn't long-necked. Rather, the rear portion of the head is elongated and tubular. Females have short heads, and the function of the long head in their mates is not understood.* (Edward S. Ross)

27 *bottom. The metallic scales of a* Cyphus germari *mimic the foliage on which it sits in the Brazilian rainforest. Snout beetles and weevils comprise the largest family of insects, the Curculionidae, with some 40,000 species worldwide. Generally, the head is elongated into a down-curved beak or "snout," with pincerlike mandibles at the tip. Many curculionines are serious agricultural pests, among them the infamous Cotton Boll Weevil* (Anthonomus grandis). *But because they are attracted to specific plants, some species have been useful in the biological control of noxious weeds.* (Kjell B. Sandved)

27

28 *and* **29** *bottom. Always pugnacious when the attention of a female is involved, two male European Stag Beetles* (Lucanus cervus) *battle with their long, antlerlike mandibles. Ancient oak forests are the haunt of this spectacular species, which is protected by law in several countries. Male European Stag Beetles attain a length of three inches; females, with much smaller jaws, are half that size. The larva feeds on rotting wood for a full five years; another year passes before an adult beetle emerges from the pupa, to feed on sap flowing from wounds in the tree bark.* (*28* René Pierre Bille; *29 bottom* Pierre Pilloud/Jacana)

29 *top. A male stag beetle,*
Prosopocoilus savagei, *in the Congo
forest. The highly developed
mandibles of both male and female
stag beetles are powerful enough to
draw blood from a human finger—
hence their other common name,
"pinching bug."* (Edward S. Ross)

30 *overleaf. The slender shape,
shiny blue-black body, and red
head identify the Clover Stem Borer*
(Languria mozardi), *one of the lizard
beetles. Widespread east of the
Rocky Mountains, the Clover Stem
Borer is a minor pest; its larvae
bore into the stems of clover,
alfalfa, and other legumes, causing
them to swell and break apart.*
(Robert W. Mitchell)

32. *A red-blue checkered beetle explores the sepal of a wild iris in a Michigan marsh. This pretty species, three-eighths of an inch long, feeds on pollen and tiny insects such as thrips. Its larvae attach themselves to bees and wasps and are carried to the nests, where they eat the hosts' young.* (John Shaw)

33 *top. A Spotted Savage Beetle* (Omophron tessellatum) *scurries over the sandy shore of a Michigan pond. As its name suggests, this one-eighth-inch-long insect is a voracious nocturnal predator. During the day, savage beetles congregate in burrows in wet sand or mud along lakes and streams.* (Larry West)

33 *bottom. Standing upside down, pushing herself along with powerful forelegs, a female scarab beetle* (Scarabaeus sp.) *rolls a dung ball toward her excavated brood chamber. Eggs will be laid in these pellets, which provide food for the hatching larvae. An inch-long scarab beetle can shape and move a hard ball of manure the size of an apple. Important scavengers, scarab beetles recycle countless tons of animal waste, carrion, and decaying vegetable matter.* (Jean Paul Hervy/Jacana)

34 *overleaf. When the morning glory blossom closes for the night, this iridescent Mexican scarab beetle will use it as a "sleeping bag," emerging when the flower conveniently reopens at dawn. Most famous of the 20,000 species in the family Scarabaeidae is the Sacred Scarab* (Scarabaeus sacer), *an insect possessing divine symbolism in the myths of ancient Egypt.* (Harry N. Darrow)

38 *overleaf. Spotted Ladybug Beetles* (Ceratomegilla maculata) *glean minute insects from the blossoms of spring beauty, one of the earliest wildflowers to emerge in the deciduous woodlands of southern Michigan. Ladybug beetles are extraordinarily prolific: a single female may lay a thousand eggs, and since the entire life cycle takes only a few weeks, several broods a year are produced even in temperate habitats. As an example of the ladybug's benefit to man, one larva will consume 3,000 larval scale insects and perhaps a hundred adults.* (Larry West)

37. *On a warm spring morning, dozens of Convergent Ladybug Beetles* (Hippodamia convergens) *swarm over a fencepost along a rural California road. In California, vast numbers of ladybug beetles gather on favorite wintering spots in mountain canyons, hibernating in huge aggregations beneath leaves and snow. Entrepreneurs gather them by the bushel for sale to citrus growers, for the ladybugs prey voraciously on harmful aphids.* (Thomas W. Davies)

36. *A black X across the bright orange elytra—the hard forewings that protect a beetle's hind, flight wings—identifies the Swamp Milkweed Leaf Beetle* (Labidomera clivicollis). *Found across much of North America, this colorful half-inch beetle feeds on the foliage and flowers of various kinds of milkweed, but especially swamp milkweed with its rose-purple flowers. In winter, adults hibernate in the shriveled, woolly leaves of mullein, a common roadside weed.* (Robert P. Carr)

40. *In this two-hour time exposure, a mangrove in a Malaysian estuary is lit up like a Christmas tree by the blinking of fireflies,* Pteroptyx malaccae. *There are 1,300 species of fireflies worldwide, and since their flashing is a means of attracting mates, the rhythm, timing, and color vary from species to species. These Asian lightning bugs, for instance, give off ninety double-flashes per minute—in perfect synchrony. Most female fireflies are wingless and resemble the larval form.* (Ivan Polunin)

41 *top. The "glowworm" of a familiar old song could be either a flightless female or a firefly larva, which has a luminous organ at its tail—and may even glow inside the egg! As is typical of firefly larvae, this Malaysian specimen* (Lucernuta *sp.*) *feeds on snails, slugs, and other invertebrate animals. Most adult fireflies, however, never eat.* (Ivan Polunin)

41 *bottom. On summer nights across eastern North America, small children catch jars full of Pyralis Fireflies* (Photinus pyralis). *Stored in an organ at the tip of the beetle's abdomen are a pigment, called luciferin, and an enzyme, luciferase. When oxygen and luciferase are combined, a catalytic reaction causes the luciferin to produce cold light. The firefly times its signals by regulating the flow of oxygen to its luminous organ.* (Edward R. Degginger)

42 *overleaf. A Stumpy Longhorn* (Anoplodera vittata) *feasts on the abundant pollen of a wild rose in a Michigan meadow. Beetles of the family Cerambycidae are popular with collectors, for many of the 20,000 species are brightly colored, and their antennae—the "horns"—can be several times longer than the insects' slender bodies. The wood-boring grubs of long-horned beetles often cause serious damage to fruit and shade trees.* (John Shaw)

44. *Shield bug nymphs (family Scutellaridae) clump around their eggs in a Malayan rainforest. To survive, shield bugs require a supply of bacteria which they store in intestinal pouches—the nymphs obtain a lifetime supply from deposits made on and between the eggs by the female when she lays the eggs. Shield bugs are protected from predators by repugnant secretions that issue from slits atop the abdomen. Their bright colors advertise their bad taste to birds.* (Edward S. Ross)

Cicadas, Hoppers, and Other Beaked Bugs

In his diary entry for March 26, 1835, Charles Darwin reported a drama in miniature during a meal aboard H.M.S. *Beagle*. Darwin had brought to the table to show the assembled officers an inch-long wingless black bug he had caught at Iquique in northern Chile. From its flatness he knew that the bug was even hungrier than the men. "When placed on the table, and though surrounded by people, if a finger was presented, the bold insect would immediately protrude its sucker, make a charge, and if allowed, draw blood. No pain was caused by the wound. It was curious to watch its body during the act of sucking, as in less than ten minutes it changed from being as flat as a wafer to a globular form. This one feast, for which the *benchuca* was indebted to one of the officers, kept it fat during four whole months; but, after the first fortnight, it was quite ready to have another suck." The *benchuca* of the story was *Triatoma infestans*, of the family Reduviidae, an insect that is widespread throughout western South America.

Fully 95,000 related insects make a living in a similar way. They drive their sharp mouthparts into some animal or plant, and then imbibe liquid nourishment as external parasites. Some, such as the spined soldier bugs (*Podisus* spp., Pentatomidae), earn our gratitude by stabbing noxious caterpillars and sucking them to death. Others, such as the aphids (Aphididae), mealybugs (Pseudococcidae), scale insects (Coccidae), and leafhoppers (Cicadellidae), attack a plant we value, draining its life juices as surely as though they were agents of some disease.

Indeed, many of these creatures transfer bacteria and viruses from infected hosts to healthy ones, spreading contagion like a plague.

These beak-bearers fall into two natural groups. One type, known collectively as the "true bugs" (order Hemiptera), has its beak arising from the front of the head, giving best leverage for an inward stab. The other type (order Homoptera), with no inclusive common name, contains the aphids, scale insects, cicadas, leafhoppers, and myriad others; in this type, the beak arises from the rear of the head and is often concealed between the bases of the legs. Although weaker, these rear-beaked kinds are experts at insinuating their sharp mouthparts into a plant to reach the tubes through which the desired nourishment flows.

Many of these insects take nourishment from one kind of plant early in the summer season, where they produce several generations of females but no males. Then they transfer to a different kind of vegetation, multiplying there a while before generating a population of both males and females. The mated females lay fertilized eggs which alone survive the winter. Thus, the Rosy Apple Aphid (*Dysaphis plantaginea*) hatches from eggs on apple trees and produces several wingless generations by virgin birth. With the color change in the pear-shaped adult from rosy brown or purple to brownish-green comes the development of wings, which carry the females in July to plantains—mere weeds in the orchard. There, several additional generations of wingless females follow one another before winged females appear in autumn, fly to apple trees, and produce wingless males and females that mate. The pale green eggs, which turn shiny black, are hidden in crevices in the bark of trees.

Root aphids (*Pemphigus* spp.), whose body colors are often concealed under a whitish dust, also live by sucking juices. They multiply on trees during the spring months, then fly or are carried by attentive ants to reach the roots of wild grasses and cereal crop plants. Concealed underground where ant galleries have exposed a root, the aphids go through further generations of wingless females. When winged females appear in autumn, the ants bring them to the surface and let them fly back to the trees, where wingless males and females develop, mate, and produce fertilized eggs that survive the winter.

The reward the ants seek for their role is sweet honeydew. The aphids exude this liquid as a surplus of sugar solution taken from the plant, while retaining the scarcer amounts of amino acids—the raw materials for producing proteins. Honeydew comes only from sucking insects whose beaks penetrate the phloem cells through which the plant conducts its most elaborated, precious products from photosynthesis. Beak-bearing insects that push their mouthparts into the sapwood obtain a more dilute solution and have nothing to give away; ants ignore them.

Every continent except Australia is inhabited by beak-bearers that make a watery environment for their soft bodies without leaving dry land. We meet these spittle insects, or froghoppers (Cercopidae), in fields and woodlands, where they stand on some weed or grass stem or pine branch. They imbibe a plant's juice while bubbling air through the excess liquid and stabilizing the froth with a glandular secretion. The bubbles last as though they had been beaten into egg white.

Leafhoppers (Cicadellidae) and treehoppers (Membracidae) leap like froghoppers when threatened, but produce no froth at any age. Some of these insects wear beautiful colors, such as the lengthwise brilliant bands on the Scarlet-and-Green Leafhopper (*Graphocephala coccinea*) of northeastern North America, or the bright yellow with black spots of the European Pasture Leafhopper (*Cicadula sexnotata*). The treehoppers rely for their safety upon their uniform green or brown color and an astonishing resemblance to spines and thorns, which make them appear inedible while they take nourishment from some soft stem.

Equally compact in body form but several sizes larger are the cicadas (Cicadidae), the noisiest of all insects. Most of the world's 1,500 species are large and heavy-bodied. Britain has only one cicada, *Cicadetta montana*, but about 75 are native to North America. Three among those 75 are now recognized as the Methuselahs of the insect world. They sing such similar songs in the same areas that for years they were believed to be a single species known as the Periodical Cicada (*Magicicada septendecim*); the Latin for *seventeen* refers to the fact that these amazing insects spend seventeen years underground, burrowing as immature nymphs and feeding on the sap in tree roots, before they emerge from the soil. Then within a few hours and usually before sunrise, they clamber up the nearest tree, split their nymphal skins, and emerge as winged adults. They have just a few weeks to live as adults while starting off the next generation.

Some of these synchronized populations (broods) are large and occupy major areas. Other broods are small, encountered in areas of less than one hundred square miles. Broods that are separated in emergence time by four years or more tend to overlap in geographical distribution, whereas those separated by only one year border each other with no overlap. Some places have as many as seven different broods. Southern broods have a shorter cycle, maturing in thirteen years. Ecologists regard the timing of emergence at long intervals as a beneficial strategy. It saturates the appetites of the predators in a few days, and allows the main population to call and mate without interference.

The sound-producing organs of the cicadas show a unique design. On the underside of the abdomen is a pair of taut membranes. Muscles inside the body cause the membranes to vibrate, while air sacs near by act as resonators. These sacs take up so much space inside the insect that its digestive tract is curled, instead of straight.

The call of the Dogday Harvestfly (*Tibicen canicularis*), a singer from coniferous and mixed woods in northeastern North America, has been described as "a powerful, high-pitched, raucous scream, somewhat like the sound made by a circular saw going through a board." It proves to have a carrier wave at 74,000 cycles per second, modulated vigorously between 184 and 360 times per second. The sound affects the human ears as does a tone on the piano in the octave between F-sharp below middle C and the next F-sharp lower still.

A more northern cicada, *Okanagana rimosa,* is like the Dogday Harvestfly in needing only one to three years of subterranean feeding before maturity. Males of *Okanagana* produce a carrier wave at 8,100 cycles and pulse it regularly about 355 times per second, which is close to F-sharp below middle C. In the woodland we listen to these calls on a hot summer day and distinguish them easily. With binoculars we can often make out the singers themselves, partway up the tree trunks.

In the rainforests of tropical America, as in those of Malaya and Borneo, the cicadas sound forth at the break of day and at the end, with calls louder than those we notice when the sun is high. In Australia, the primitive Alpine Cicada (*Tettigarcta crinita*), like its close relative *T. tomentosa* in Tasmania, seems strictly nocturnal, hiding beneath bark all day. In these species, both male and female are equipped for sound production.

American Indians of the southwestern United States and Mexico learned long ago how to manufacture a crimson dye (carmine) by collecting Cochineal Bugs (*Dactylopius confusus*) from prickly pears and other cacti, drying the bugs, and extracting a water-soluble pigment. Conspicuous clusters of these often cover large areas of the cactus like a white furry rug. Since carmine dye washes out of cloth, it has been replaced by more permanent pigments except where Indians continue their ancient ways.

Some of the lanternflies (Fulgoridae) are rather strange, appearing as though—as someone once claimed—their growth had gone to their heads. Most grotesque is the rare *Lantenaria phosphorea* of the Amazon forest near the Andes. Sometimes it may be luminous; it associates in the jungle with luminous bacteria, against which it may sometimes rub, producing this appearance. The insect's head has a great hollow projection the size of an unshelled peanut, and shaped much like an alligator's head: markings along each side look like the reptile's teeth, and the bulge on top, its eyes. The insect's own eyes are almost hidden under the rear of the head projection, through which a loop of the digestive tract extends for no known reason. *Lantenaria*, with a wing expanse of six inches, becomes a prize to be better understood.

A surer reason for continuing to refer to lanternflies by their actual common name is that the Chinese collect masses of flocculent wax from the young of the Candlefly (*Fulgora candelaria*) of Southeast Asia, with which they make candles for home lighting. As an adult, this insect is over an inch long as it rests with its red-on-yellow spotted green forewings laid back flat over its body, concealing its black-tipped red hind wings. Its brownish-red head cone thrusts forward, with a rounded knob at the tip.

The smaller lanternflies over much of the world have wing colors and patterns so bright that the collector is tempted to spread them like moths, the better to admire the display. It is often easy to forget that they are homopterans, efficient external parasites on plants or predators on small animals. Seen from above, the beak does not show at all. It consists of a flexible upper lip, or labrum, curled into the shape of a tube slit along the rear, which grasps and guides the four lancets that penetrate the food supply, then fit together in parts to direct the outward flow of saliva and the inward flow of nourishment. The upper lip stays outside the wound, reassembling the lancets into a tight array for storage after they are withdrawn from the plant.

Why these insects should be rewarded for rivalling the rainbow of colors or for drawing such attention to themselves remains one of Nature's secrets. The explanation will probably come to someone who intently observes a bright lanternfly without disturbing its daily routine.

The largest of the beak-bearers, some of them 4½ inches long, live in freshwater shallows. These giant water bugs (Belostomatidae) creep or swim slowly among submerged vegetation and ambush fish, tadpoles, or other insects. The first spring brood of giant water bugs may survive to maturity, but thereafter they are their own worst enemies. The next generation cannibalize one another, leaving only a few to overwinter. Most of these bugs are tropical, but North America has several that are found as far north as Canada.

Any giant water bug can deliver a painful stab to a barefooted wader and earn itself a reputation as a "toe-biter." Smaller ones, rarely more than an inch and a half in length, inhabit shallow ponds west of the Rocky Mountains, across southern Canada and into New England. It is marvelous to witness how they give their eggs more than usual protection. After mating, the female seizes the male and holds him firmly until she is ready to lay her eggs. Then she cements the eggs in a solid array, all upended, atop his back, and makes sure they are securely attached. For a while after she releases him, he skulks among the bottom vegetation and tries to dislodge his burden. Later he comes to the surface and rocks his body, washing water rich in oxygen between the eggs. Not until the young have escaped through the upper end of the eggs does water soften the cement, allowing the male to go free. Frequently his first move without a load is to find another female and become a living incubator again.

The quiet waters in which aquatic hemipterans live frequently become stagnant, with virtually no dissolved oxygen. These insects then need to reach atmospheric air and refill the ventilation system inside the body. Many do so by raising the abdominal tip through the surface film. The water scorpions (Nepidae) reach up almost an inch with a pair of slender abdominal extensions pressed close together to form a tube, while the insect itself watches for small prey it can snatch and kill.

Looking into the shallows, we often spy a lurking bug, a half-inch backswimmer (Notonectidae), which spends almost its entire life upside down. Its coloration, somewhat like that of a fish, provides countershading: its black underside is toward the sky, its pale wings face the stream bottom. A backswimmer adjusts its buoyancy, rising or sinking slowly through the water. The two longest legs (the middle pair) extend as sculling oars. They help alert the insect to any ripple or vibration in the water. The backswimmer turns and rows toward a flying ant that has fallen into the pond and is struggling at the surface. Juices from inside the ant become a meal for the backswimmer. A tadpole will serve it just as well, for the backswimmer is a predator and ready for whatever comes along. For defense, it can use its beak effectively to stab, thereby earning the name "water wasp" in Europe.

Patrolling the surface of almost any pond or slow stream are water striders (members of the families Gerridae and Microveliidae), whose second and third pairs of legs are extremely long and slender. Extended feet bear short, waxy hairs that allow the insect to stand or scull on the water surface film. A strider keeps alert for vibrations that could inform it of the location of some small creature that has fallen into the water—potential prey. Other vibrations, created by the striders themselves, serve as a kind of communication: they attract females to males that have found a suitable place to deposit eggs, or repel rival males without recourse to battle.

Safely on land, we may take a really close look at the cosmopolitan Tarnished Plant Bug (*Lygus lineolaris*, Mirandae) and see that its shiny surface, only a quarter-inch in length, is handsomely patterned in yellow and dark stripes and brown to green stripes.

These features blur at a short distance and help the insect "vanish" without hiding.

For sheer elegance of outline and patterns of color, few insects can compete with the shield-shaped stink bugs (Pentatomidae). The Latin American species *Brachytethus rubromaculatus*, for example, is blue-black with large red spots, and *Chalcocoris rutilans* of tropical Africa is bright green with red and yellow markings. With a body more than an inch in length, the ochre back of Borneo's *Catacanthus incarnatus* bears iridescent green crosswise markings that match the color of its head, legs, and antennae. For contrast, the Green Soldier Bug (*Acrosternum hilare*), widespread in the United States and Canada, is all bright green except for narrow spots of yellow, orange, red, and black along its sides and below. The Harlequin Cabbage Bug (*Murgantia histrionica*) of North America wears a clown's garb of orange-red, black, and yellow. Often we meet a boldly patterned stinkbug standing motionless with a large caterpillar impaled upon its beak. Such a sight reminds us that the insect's diet includes more than the juices of garden and orchard plants in whose welfare we have a stake.

Fantasy rather than aesthetics seems to rule the shapes in which the leaf-footed bugs and squash bugs (Coreidae) appear. The giant *Thasus gigas*, of Mexico and adjacent areas of the United States, is almost two inches long; it has red-and-black swollen knobs on its out-thrust antennae—not at the tip, but part way out. The same colors also stripe its sturdy legs. These hues appear again conspicuously on the hind tibiae of the South American *Diactor bilineatus*, a leaf-footed bug that is always a surprise when it settles suddenly beside you upon some leaf, intent on finding there either abundant sap or the life juice from some insect prey. The Squash Bug (*Anasa tristis*) of North America, slightly more than half an inch in length, appears plain leaf-green by comparison. This insect seems almost a sign of spring when we find it in the fallen leaves among which it has spent the winter.

53–55. *It is midnight in Texas, and the nymph of a Great Western Cicada* (Tibicen dorsata) *has emerged from the ground below a Chinese elm. The nymph has lived there for three years, feeding on the roots of the tree on which its metamorphosis into an adult will take place. An hour after the exoskeleton begins to split along the back, the wings of the cicada become hard and the insect can fly away. By dawn, dozens of empty nymphal skins will be hanging from the bark of these trees, which are a favorite of this beautiful species. The Great Western Cicada, which has a 4½-inch wingspan, is found in the southern Rocky Mountains; its song is an intense whine. There is a new generation of this species each summer, but in eastern states, a single locality will be treated to an emergence of periodical cicadas* (Magicicada spp.) *only once in every thirteen or seventeen years.* (Robert W. Mitchell)

56. *Planthoppers* (Acanalonia *sp.*) *suck sap from the stem of Queen Anne's lace in a New Jersey field. Less than three-eighths of an inch long, these wedge-shaped insects with their protruding heads can be found by the dozens on a single plant. Worldwide there are some 5,000 species of planthoppers in the family Fulgoridae. Nearly all of them are accomplished "hoppers," and many sport bright colors.* (C. A. Latch/Marcon Photo)

57. *Mint leaves in a New York garden lure Scarlet-and-Green Leafhoppers* (Graphocephala coccinea). *Powerful jumpers, these strikingly marked insects are known as "sharpshooters" because of their habit of forcibly expelling a drop of clear liquid about once every second while they feed on plant juices. This "honeydew," a sweetish mixture of unused plant sap and body waste, attracts flies, bees, wasps, and ants. Plants on which leafhoppers feed often wilt and drop leaves, because the insects inject saliva that blocks tubes essential for the movement of sap.* (Charles Krebs)

58 *overleaf. A coreid bug (family* Coreidae) *draws sap from the flower of a platanillo, a member of the banana family and a common understory plant in tropical forests. A close relative of this Costa Rican specimen is the Squash Bug* (Anasa tristis), *a common and destructive garden pest across North America. Both adults and larvae attack cucumbers, squash, pumpkins, and melons, and the larvae feed as well on beans, peas, and corn. Several generations of Squash Bugs are produced a year, the adults overwintering among the huge, withered leaves.* (Edward S. Ross)

60. *This quarter-inch treehopper (Umbonia* sp.*) is also called a "thorn bug," for obvious reasons. The pronotum—the upper part of the skeleton of the prothorax—extends backward into a sharp dorsal spine and two lateral spines. Some observers consider the thornlike shape a form of disguise. But a bird that tries to swallow such a pain-inflicting morsel is unlikely to forget the experience, and is reminded of it by the thorn bug's bright colors. (Stephen J. Krasemann/DRK Photo)*

61. *Thousands of species of treehoppers (family Membracidae) occur worldwide, but in the New World tropics the development of the pronotum has produced creatures of the most bizarre shapes imaginable. One such is this Costa Rican specimen, of the genus Bocydium, flaunting its pawnbroker's balls. Wrote one prominent entomologist, "Proponents of the school of evolutionary thought who claim that every plant and animal structure must be of some definite benefit will have a hard time explaining these treehoppers."* (John Shaw)

62 *overleaf. Mere specks to the naked eye, whitefly nymphs (family Aleyrodidae) feed on a bromeliad leaf in a rainforest in Colombia. Attached to the host plant by a fringe of fragile, waxy filaments, these immobile larvae suck up juices through mouthparts that drill into the leaf tissue. The winged adults, about one-sixteenth of an inch long, are covered with waxy dust secreted by glands on the underside of the abdomen. Whiteflies are commonly found on greenhouse plants.* (Kjell B. Sandved)

64 and **65.** *Two species of red bugs or cotton-stainers* (Dysdercus *spp.*) *from Southeast Asia demonstrate the characteristic back-to-back mating position of true bugs of the order Hemiptera; the mating pair easily walks about while joined. The bright colors of red bugs, or fire bugs, of the family Pyrrhocoridae advertise their bad taste to hungry birds. Some species of* Dysdercus *are serious pests; they feed on cotton bolls, staining the fibers, causing distortion of the boll, and spreading fungus spores. But the cotton-stainers can be easily controlled without resorting to chemical pesticides, simply by turning chickens loose in cotton fields.* (Both Edward S. Ross)

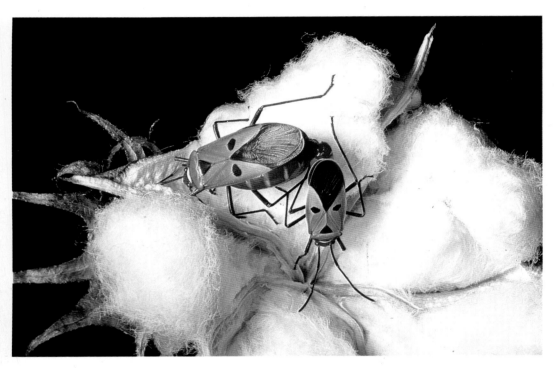

66 *overleaf. An ambush bug,* Phymata erosa, *lurks among the tiny flowers of a goldenrod cluster on the coast of Maine. Almost invisible in the yellow and green mass of its favorite hideaway, the half-inch ambush bug has forelegs adapted for seizing and holding prey—Honeybees, butterflies, day-flying moths, and wasps—from which it sucks the juices.* (Dwight R. Kuhn)

68, 69 *top and bottom. Because of their tremendous reproductive capacity, aphids or plant lice of the family Aphididae form one of the most ubiquitous and economically important groups of insects. Parthenogenesis, by females alone, is the primary mode of reproduction, but in late summer both males and females appear and leave fertilized eggs that overwinter while the rest of the population perishes. Female aphids do not lay eggs, but give birth to nymphs in which the embryos of the next generation are already forming. Such exponential growth explains why these tiny insects, less than one-eighth of an inch long, can be a serious agricultural problem, especially in orchards. Fortunately, their numbers are kept in reasonable check by predators, especially ladybug beetles. Aphids exude a sweet liquid or honeydew on which ants and other insects feed; indeed, some ants store aphid eggs in their nests during the winter and transport the insects to a food plant in spring.* (68 Edward S. Ross; 69 *top* Dwight R. Kuhn; 69 *bottom* Charles Krebs)

70 *overleaf. A female Parent-bug* (Elasmucha grisea) *attends her brood on a birch leaf in Denmark. For two centuries this bug has been known to exhibit parental care for its eggs and younger larvae. The female lays a compact, diamond-shaped mass of thirty to forty eggs on a birch leaf, covering them with her body for as long as three weeks until they all have hatched. The larvae remain clustered, with the female in attendance, for ten days, until the first molt occurs. Throughout the second nymphal stage, the young will follow her as she moves freely about. Her protection is not merely passive; the Parent-bug will interpose herself between an intruder and her brood.* (Søren Breiting/Biofoto)

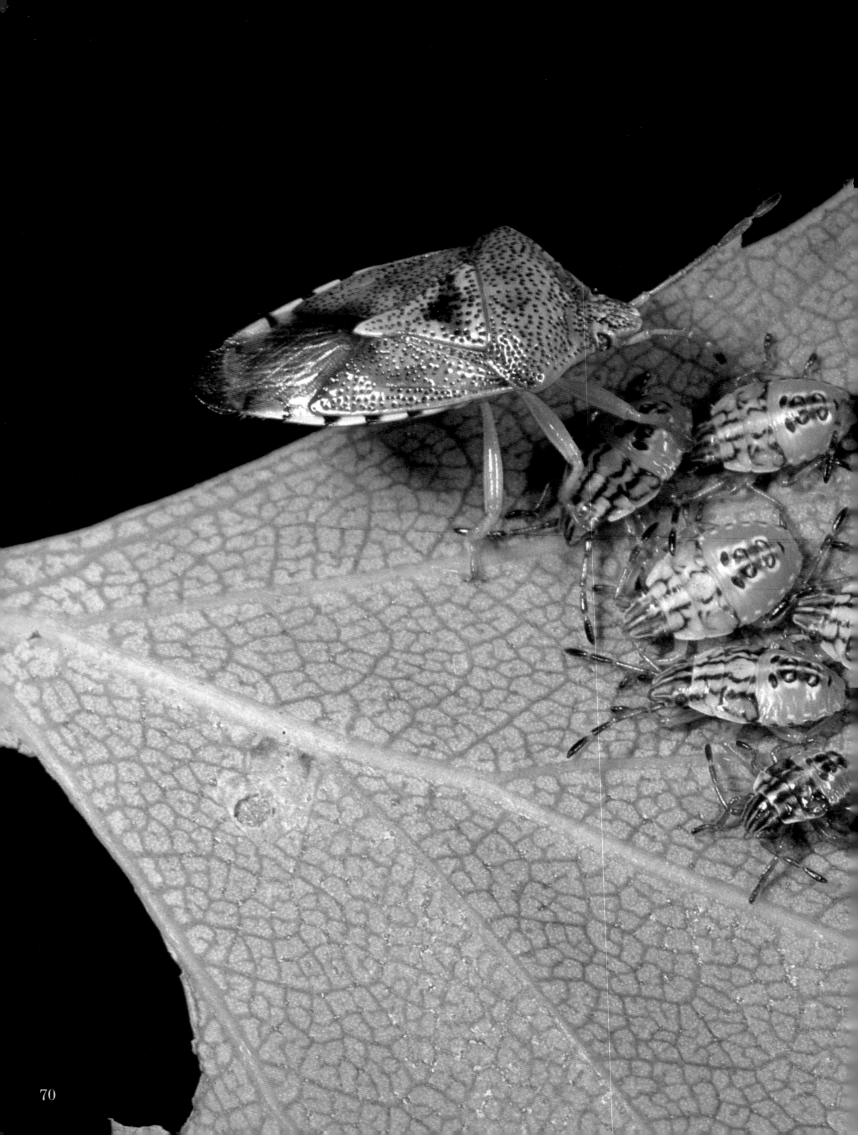

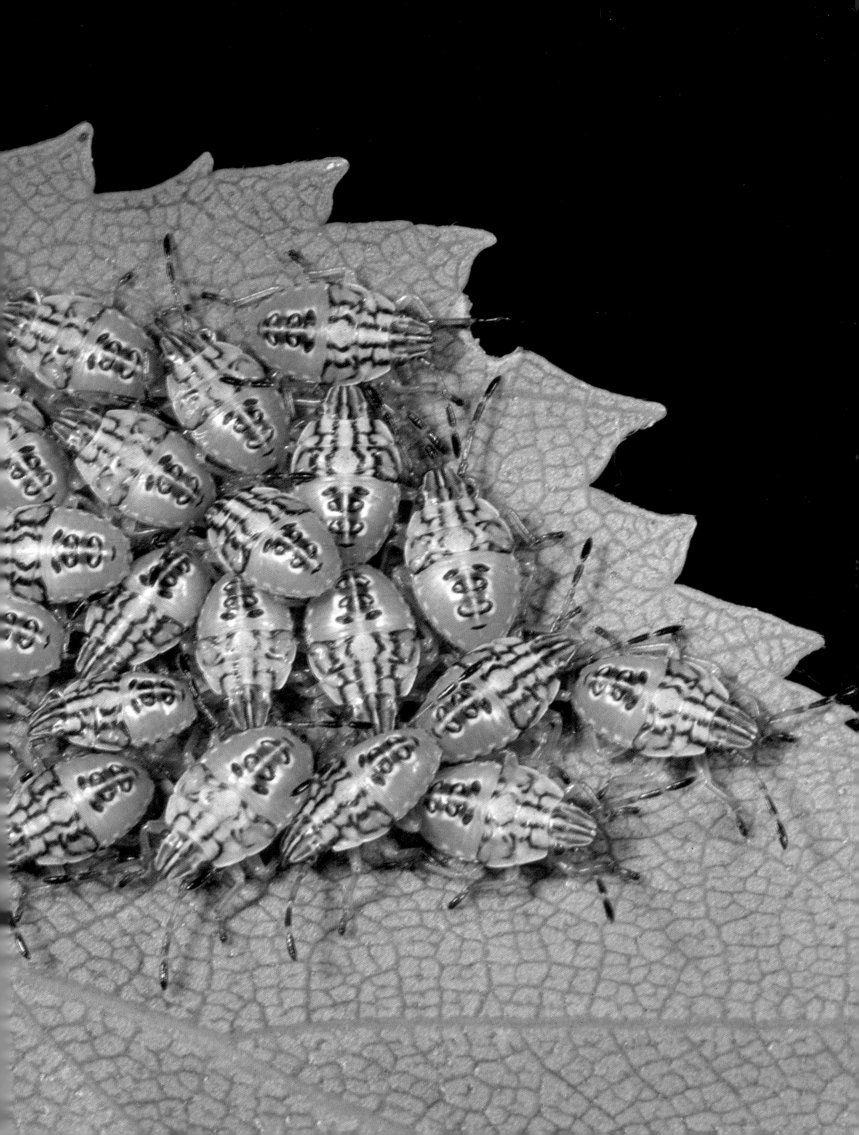

72. *Primitive, wingless creatures that may be as small as a pinhead, and no larger than a quarter-inch, springtails are named for a special organ, called a furcula, that is folded forward under the abdomen. When a catch is released, the furcula snaps back and catapults the springtail several inches into the air. Worldwide, there are 2,000 species of springtails, more than 300 in North America. Crawling over a decaying oak leaf, this springtail (Orchesella sp.) belongs to the largest family, the Entomobryidae, whose members inhabit forest litter, humus, fungi, and rotting bark. (Patrick Lorne/ Jacana)*

Parasites and Primitives

Among creatures great and small, it is often the inconspicuous ones—such as the elusive parasites and the wingless, unseen primitive insects—that have the greatest impact on civilization.

On some South Pacific islands, as in tropical America and Africa, a mother or medicine man often checks for lice on a person who seems sick. The presence of lice on the head means that the patient has a normal body temperature and may soon recover; a fever induces the parasites to shift to a new host. Similarly, if the temperature of the body falls a few degrees, these creatures desert it. The spread of bubonic plague, in fact, is credited to the rapid transfer of fleas from fevered rats to people, creating epidemics of the dread disease.

The sensitivity to temperature shown by lice, fleas, mosquitoes, and other insects that feed on blood is made evident by the differences between individual people or between other kinds of animals that contain blood. Usually the same person attracts lice, fleas, mosquitoes, chiggers, or other pests. When out walking in the evening with a companion, the person who radiates an inner warmth becomes the center of a cloud of pests—a distinction that is rarely appreciated. The victim slaps at the tormentors, raising the already high skin temperature by this exertion, and bringing more and more hungry mosquitoes to the scene. No insects may bother the victim's cooler companion, for even when alone, such people usually attract few parasites. But if they have a fever, or exercise and raise the skin temperature above normal, they too become parasite prone.

White skin, or white clothing such as people often wear in the tropics, may serve as protection from insects, including mosquitoes, that find their victims through the heat they radiate. But white skin or garments may form easy targets for horse flies, deer flies, and others that hunt by sight, and for stinging insects, such as wasps. In the wild Darién Province of Panama, the Chocó Indians explained that they stain their pale skins as black as possible not only because they could thus remain unseen, but also because fewer insects bite them when their bodies blend with the jungle shadows.

Reliance upon sensitivity to heat gets some parasites into unsuitable situations. In a Mexican market, by walking too close to stalls where pigs were waiting to be purchased, we became the unexpected hosts to Hog Lice (*Haematopinus suis*), which crossed the pavement and climbed our legs. Our odor did not suit them and they did not bite, but they surely made us feel unwashed. No such distinction saves us nearer to home in places where a Dog Flea (*Ctenocephalides canis*) or Cat Flea (*C. felix*)—both a mere eighth of an inch long—cannot find a proper host. The parasite will leap to us and take one bite after another before searching for a dog or cat.

The Human Flea (*Pulex irritans*), which can transmit bubonic plague after a blood meal from an infected person, can live and multiply on dogs, coyotes, cats, pigs, mules and horses, deer, and various rodents, as well as primates. Part of the requirement seems to be that the host have a nest or a favorite sleeping site of some kind. The larval fleas can scavenge among the organic debris in the nest.

The 1,600 kinds of fleas (Siphonaptera) on Earth grow no more than a quarter-inch in length, with extremely narrow bodies as adults, letting them slip easily between the hairs of a mammal. Three piercing stylets in the mouth permit the creature to stab through skin and reach the blood. Some have small compound eyes that supplement the short antennae as sense organs. Elongation of the first segment of each leg confers upon the creature its extraordinary power to leap a foot or more into the air. All of these abilities are gained during the pupal transformation, which takes place in a neat silken cocoon spun by the whitish, maggotlike larva.

A louse is a very different creature, a creepy companion that is too fastidious to accept a host different from the one on which it has fed through immaturity to adulthood. The sucking lice (Anoplura), such as Hog Lice and Human Lice (*Pediculus humanus*—the body louse; *P. capitis*—the head louse), feed repeatedly, making a fresh puncture each time. Three tiny stylets are pushed into the skin through a sort of sleevelike beak, which is turned inside out during the operation, exposing microscopic hooks that hold on to the host until the meal is finished. Usually each leg has a clamplike structure with which the louse can cling to a hair. The chewing lice (Mallophaga), such as those that infest chickens, are more bristly, with larger heads and abdomens; they spend their entire existence on or near some host whose dead skin or feathers supply their food.

Wingless booklice (Psocoptera) infest many houses, where they feed on the glue used in book bindings. Occasionally, a booklouse astonishes us by creeping slowly across an open page. Its long, threadlike antennae, bulging head with prominent compound eyes, bulbous abdomen, and short midsection with legs do not tell us whether it is immature or an adult, for the creature undergoes no pupal transformation. Winged individuals usually await discovery on the bark of a tree, where they cluster in little groups; they are called barklice because they nibble on bark or other dry plant material. They do no damage with their minute chewing mouthparts and seldom fly, even when disturbed. They escape by dropping from any support and standing in litter on the ground, motionless and inconspicuous.

The Silverfish (*Lepisma saccharina*), half an inch long, is a worldwide household pest, a bristletail (Thysanura) that eats dried cereals, flour, starch, and glue so avidly it can skim the shiny surface from quality coated paper or destroy the binding of a cherished book. Almost uniquely among insects that we encounter domestically, it attains its wingless maturity with no change in body form or food habits; nor does it take time after a brief molt to become expert in some new behavior. Its equal in destructive abilities is the mottled gray-and-brown Firebrat (*Thermobia domestica*) of Eurasia, which has spread everywhere that people leave crumbs and food scraps near cooking and heating devices.

Some of the world's most bizarre small insects find little to interest them in human enterprises. To

75

discover a social group of webspinners (Embioptera), we may go to the tropics, or the American South, or the Far West, and hunt for their silken galleries in clumps of moss, patches of lichens, under stones, or in crevices in bark. There the young and the adult females use their chewing mouthparts to eat decaying plant material. The males—the only ones to develop wings—are carnivorous.

Thrips (Thysanoptera) are easier to find, for they creep into flowers and find space for their slim bodies among the florets of a daisy. Generally they curl the abdomen over the back as they crawl on very short legs, and seem scarcely more than dark particles of dirt. The females use a sawlike ovipositor to slit the stems of wheat, cotton, and citrus. Many remain wingless for life. Others develop four narrow wings with distinctive fringes that let the insect flutter in a breeze and be carried aloft for hours and miles. Most of the time they remain among the least conspicuous insects, without sacrificing their ability to multiply, either by virgin birth or regular mating, when their Lilliputian world offers them the amenities they need. They escape its harshness by overwintering in the soil.

On a winter field trip, we see tiny dark blue motes cavorting or forming dark patches on white snow. These Snow Fleas (*Achorutes nivicola*) are not insects at all, but collembolans. Also inconspicuous most of the year is the Seashore Springtail (*Anurida maritima*), dark blue to slate-gray, which ventures out on the surface of tide pools when the waves have retreated. Huge clusters of these creatures are often found nestled in air pockets when the tide is high. Found worldwide, they scatter their eggs among beach litter, hatch in spring, and scavenge for juices from decaying plant material all over the beach between tide marks. These creatures have only four to six abdominal segments, fewer than any insect, a fact that leads entomologists to relegate them to a class of their own.

77. Photographed on the hairs of its host on a Texas farm, this Hog Louse (Haematopinus suis) is among 250 species of wingless, bloodsucking lice that parasitize mammals, including humans. Wherever there are pigs, Hog Lice will be found in their ears or folds of the skin. Eggs are glued to hog hairs and quickly hatch; both nymphs and adult lice make a new puncture hole each time they feed. Most sucking lice belong to the family Haematopinidae, blind pests of wild and domestic animals. A few species in the family Echinophthiriidae live on marine mammals, concealed in air pockets between the hairs of seals, sea lions, and walruses. (Robert W. Mitchell)

78 overleaf. Uncountable thousands of springtails swarm over a partly submerged log at the edge of a Michigan pond. These are Snow Fleas (Achorutes nivicola), most famous of their minute kind. On warm winter days, millions of snow fleas can blacken the thawing white blanket of northern woodlands, or pepper the blinding snowfields of Arctic glaciers. (Robert P. Carr)

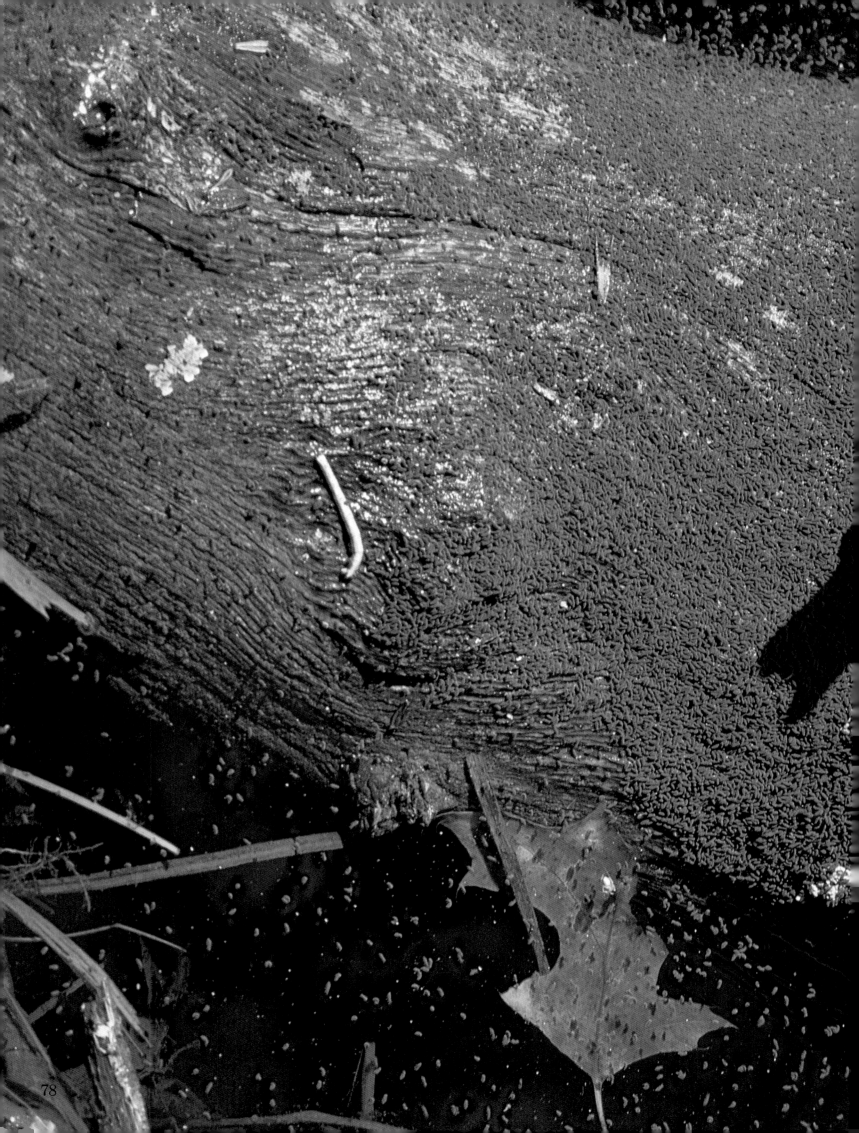

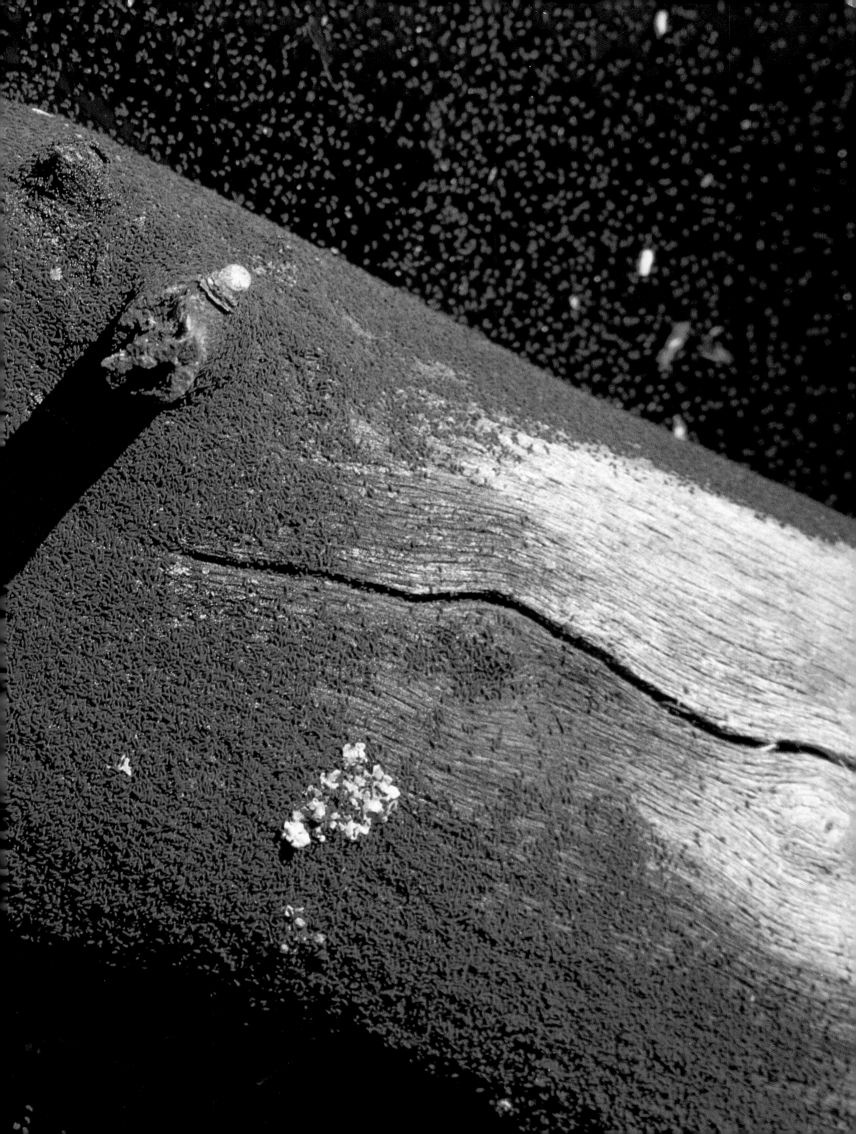

80. *Famous among entomologists are the leaf insects of Asia, close relatives of the more familiar stick insects. Typical is this female Wandering-Leaf* (Phyllium biocolatum) *from Java. Its incredibly flattened body, color, and markings, even the shape of its legs, mimic the tropical foliage. Considerably larger than the males —some are four inches long— female leaf insects are flightless but retain stubby front wings that add to the success of the masquerade. They are able to produce viable eggs that hatch into female nymphs without mating.*
(Hervé Chaumeton/Jacana)

Master Mimics

Many defenseless insects gain security at a bargain by masquerading as unappetizing parts of their natural backgrounds. An inchworm two inches long proved this at the edge of the Panamanian rainforest, where we were seated, staying as motionless as possible the better to discover native animals in their surroundings. The caterpillar, resembling a brown-streaked twig jutting from a bush a few feet away, remained undetected until it moved more quickly than usual. Abruptly, a mantis of leaf-green color materialized a short distance beyond. Leaping into the air, the mantis flew in and seized the caterpillar in its spine-studded, grasping forelegs.

Perhaps the mantis was clumsy, for the caterpillar writhed and tried to free itself. The continued commotion caught the attention of a Blue-crowned Motmot (*Momotus momota*) perched on a branch a hundred feet higher up. Down plunged the bird and snatched the mantis in its beak. Without a pause the motmot flew back to its lookout spot. As it went, we saw the caterpillar fall from the mantis' grasp, and then the wings of the mantis, broken off by the motmot, came fluttering to the ground as waste. Once more the forest edge appeared devoid of anything other than plant life. Only a momentary whir of wings, as the brightly colored motmot braked its swift descent and caught its meal, had disturbed the jungle peace.

Each of the actors in that swift drama had proved a master of self-concealment. The mantis *Choeradodis strumaria*, with its chlorophyll-green color and flaring green collar, had both the hue and the unusual outline to keep us from recognizing it and penetrating its camouflage. Like so many of its close relatives, it blended with the foliage it stood on. Quite evidently, the motmot did not recognize the mantis as food until the creature moved. The mantis did not detect the caterpillar until it swayed faster than a breeze would move a twig. The motmot in its green plumage was lost among the leaves on the branch high overhead, both before and after it dove in pursuit of the mantis. Motion destroyed the illusion that each of these animals created with stillness. As spectators, we attempted the same ruse.

The Chinese Mantis (*Tenodera aridifolia*), an Australian mantis (*Phasmida*), and the European Mantis (*Mantis religiosa*)—which has been introduced into America—are all able to stand for hours, swaying gently on their long middle and hind legs. The wings of a mantis are folded over its back, its grasping appendages held compactly beneath its head. Naturalists in the Middle Ages were reminded by its motionless pose of the prayerful attitude of a holy prophet, leading them to adopt the Greek word *mantis*, meaning a prophet, for the insect. The New World and Africa have many kinds of these strange insects. So nearly perfect is their imitation of plant parts that a leaf-eating beetle may bite hard on a mantis before discovering its identity.

Bizarre tropical mantids are often mottled with brown or other colors. A green species in South America, *Ommathoptera pictifolia*, keeps its fore wings folded over its back, exposing a single large eyespot. When alarmed by a bird, this species suddenly flares its wings, exposing a previously concealed second eyespot on the other fore wing. The two eyespots so abruptly displayed startle the bird and frighten it away, thus saving the mantis' life. The tropical forests of Southeast Asia have a one-inch pink-and-green mantis, *Hymenopus coronatus*, that blends almost perfectly with the petals of the flowers on which it waits for prey. An African mantis, *Idolium diabolicum*, resembles dead, drying leaves— as long as it stands still. This patient pose requires a minimum expenditure of energy, and the mantis can wait for weeks, if necessary, between one meal and the next. Its prey may be a butterfly, a day-flying moth, a fly or true bug, a caterpillar, or even a wasp or some other stinging insect; a mantis may take any or all of these in gradual succession. Even another mantis is acceptable prey—the ranks of these predators are well thinned.

A mantis is one of the few insects in the world that can turn their heads far enough to look over their shoulders. When the creature catches sight of some potential victim of manageable size, it turns slowly around to face in the right direction. When the large compound eyes on the small, triangular head and the grasping forelegs are aligned correctly and the prey comes within range, the mantis strikes. If it misses the first time, it can snatch again in a fraction of a second, often before an alert fly has time to make its airborne escape.

Occasionally, a mantis takes a slow step or two toward some fresh vantage point, but these insects seldom move faster than a leaf might be blown. The same slow speed is shown by a male mantis stalking a potential mate. Once within range, he must leap upon her back and land symmetrically. Otherwise she will be able to reach some part of him with her grasping legs or jaws and devour him bit by bit. Amazingly, the male's nervous system shows such functional subdivision that he can mate with the female even while she is destroying his head and beginning to consume the forward parts of his body. Gradually he becomes nourishment for the female, and a source of provision for the young that will develop from her eggs. A male that aligns himself exactly can escape to father more offspring.

Following each mating, the female mantis stands head-downward on some plant stem and extrudes as many as 200 eggs. These stay in a compact mass almost an inch in each direction, cemented together and to their support by a coating of tan froth that hardens quickly and protects the eggs all winter. They are commonly attached above the snow and exposed to the harshest weather. The covering is so firm that a bird may take an exploratory peck at the mass without doing much harm. In late spring, the mantis eggs hatch within just a few hours of one another. Pale, gangling young cling together while breezes carry away those that lose their grip. Each youngster is on its own to capture and eat whatever small flies come within reach as it wanders through the tangled summer weeds.

Predicting where a mantis will be seems impossible. Each autumn we look for these insects on the flowering heads of goldenrod, where they have often been known to stand and wait for prey—but spotting one of these graceful mimics requires patience and, sometimes, luck.

Finding a stick insect (Phasmatidae) is almost as unexpected and memorable. We came across a giant stick insect in New Zealand—the creature was twice as long as the three-inchers we find in the United States and Canada, or the slightly shorter Oriental Stick Insect (*Carausius morosus*), introduced in Britain—especially in greenhouses—where it is often adopted as a pet. Stick insects everywhere are masters of motionlessness. The slender cylindrical body may be closely applied lengthwise to a bare branch, or it may be supported on thin, long legs as the animal rocks slightly from side to side as though yielding to a breeze. All day long the stick insect may make no move, fasting until after nightfall before nibbling on edible foliage close by. By day, the still insect's green, gray, or brown colors attract no notice. No twig could be less animated.

Recently, a friend wrote us from Florida to ask about an experience he had just had. While tending a low shrub, he was suddenly squirted in the face with a milky, acrid fluid. Subsequent investigation revealed the source: a stick insect ready to repeat its defensive act. We have handled dozens of these creatures without ever witnessing such a demonstration, but know that each stick insect is well prepared with protective glands on its thorax. Occasionally, a tree full of stick insects produces copious showers of defensive fluid.

An amorous stick insect displays movements as deliberate and slow as the opening of a flower. The smaller male, upon discovering a potential mate, moves one leg in her direction every few minutes, and if she moves away, he seems reluctant to follow. If he succeeds in fertilizing her eggs, she has no need to travel to dispose of them, but simply drops them one at a time. The eggs, like seeds less than an eighth-inch in diameter, bounce from leaf to leaf until they reach the ground. There they will lie until springtime. Even if a female stick insect dies before completing her discharge of eggs, the rest of them are released as her body shrivels.

Each stick insect egg hatches at night. The feeble creature inside arches its back until a tiny circular door pops open at the end of the eggshell. Out comes the bent back, then the legs, one at a time, or a single threadlike antenna. Laboriously, the creature emerges, its leg movements still poorly coordinated. The little stick insect does its best to hurry, to climb up some stem and into the foliage, and to stand there undetected through the dangerous day, waiting for the protective darkness of night.

Tropical stick insects, together with two kinds (*Aplopus*) found in southernmost Florida, are the only ones that acquire wings as they attain maturity. Free flight may be beyond them, but when shaken from a tree they flutter until they alight safely again and can resume their all-day pose. A few of these insects in the rainforests of South America and Africa attain a length of thirteen inches; part of this great size is accounted for by the long front legs and antennae, which they hold straight ahead of the body, and which often curve down to meet the supporting branch. Many stick insects, such as *Argosarchus horridus* of New Zealand, have short, stiff spines along each side.

Closely related to the plain stick insects are the bright green leaf insects of the genus *Phyllium*, of southern and southeastern Asia. Leaf insects, which frequent the cacao trees, have amazingly broad, green abdomens and leaflike expansions of the legs, especially the front pair. The adult gains green wings that it holds flat against the back. Females cannot fly because their fore wings are broad and hardened, concealing a tiny second pair of wings fused to the back. Males have small, stumpy fore wings, but well-developed hind wings. Sometimes a leaf insect seems unable to recognize another of its own kind, unless it is of the opposite sex; one leaf insect may bite another as the two stand side by side.

The names "walkingstick" and "walking leaf" are sometimes applied to stick and leaf insects, although neither does much walking. They interest scientists because their young are capable of regenerating parts of lost legs. And both produce hatchable eggs without mating. In fact, for quite a few species, including some in North America, males are totally unknown and may not exist.

No such constraints on reproduction seem to limit the cockroaches, which, when not standing motionless, scuttle rapidly across some surface. With body thickness at a minimum and legs that swing most easily in the horizontal plane, a cockroach can slither into a narrow crack and disappear. Only its long, threadlike antennae may continue to wave back and forth as the insect samples the air beyond its hiding place for odors that might tell it what to do next. In this situation, the distinction between touching and being touched is particularly evident. An antenna can brush against objects beyond the crack without alarming the cockroach. But any contact that the movements of the antennae did not cause will send the insect scurrying away to the safety of a more secret retreat.

In his delightful *Book of Bugs*, Harvey Sutherland has a cockroach saying to the coal in the scuttle, "When you were being made, my ancestors were already well established." Cockroaches do have an immense history in the fossil record, and their successful body plan has withstood every test of time. Some credit for this success must go to a pair of extremely sensitive projections (cerci) at the posterior end of the insect's abdomen. They alert the cockroach to breezes and other events too far back to be sensed by the antennae, enabling it to perceive danger both ahead and behind.

Only the members of one genus, *Cryptocercus* in the southern Appalachians, seem to have dispensed with this rear-end warning system. They take permanent shelter in spaces inside rotting stumps and logs, the wood of which they chew up and swallow. Protozoans in their intestines, almost identical to those found in the intestines of wood-eating termites, break down the wood fibers and digest the cellulose to produce sugar, contributing to the nutrition of these woodland cockroaches.

Not all cockroaches are the furtive creatures that we are familiar with, spending most of their time lurking in crevices and relying on their antennae and cerci to warn them of approaching danger. Some are mimics as remarkable as any among their relatives the mantids, stick insects, and leaf insects. In the jungles of the Philippines, small cockroaches of the genus *Prosoplecta* exactly match the size, shape, and color of ladybug beetles of the genus *Coleophora*. The ladybugs are toxic and are avoided by predators. Unlike many other cockroaches, *Prosoplecta* wanders about over the surfaces of leaves in broad daylight, making no attempt to conceal itself. It is almost as if it knew that its colorful pattern of red with black spots makes it all but immune from the attacks of insect-eating birds.

But most cockroaches are dark reddish-brown. Some fail to develop wings but do not suffer obvious deprivation. Others acquire two pairs of wings with which they glide or flutter frantically after leaping from some high support. Knowing this, we were surprised when we met tropical cockroaches that flew quite well; a few of these were relatively huge—five inches long or more. The wingless females and the young of some kinds dive and swim effectively if disturbed, but most cockroaches rely on darkness and speed to avoid danger.

Fortunately, only a few species of cockroaches have found human foodstuffs in storage so attractive as to move in and claim a share. One widespread species is the so-called Oriental Cockroach (*Blatta orientalis*), a blackish creature; another, brown and more slender, is the German Cockroach (*Blattella germanica*). The southeastern United States is the origin of a two-inch bugaboo of many households, *Periplaneta americana;* while India, Southeast Asia, and Australia are home to the slightly different *P. australasiae.*

Cockroaches that seek human foods have a reputation for being dirty. Actually they do their best to keep themselves shiny and clean by scraping their body surfaces with their legs, then nibbling off every particle that adheres. Performing unbelievable contortions, they pass every accessible part of their feet and antennae through their mouthparts. Hours go into these grooming activities, which we overlook because they occur in the darkness of hiding places. We notice more that household cockroaches come to slake their thirst at any small leak in a plumbing system, and subdue their chronic hunger on leftover food. Even where cockroaches gain access to food before people eat it, they leave no contamination that could not ride as easily on the feet of a housefly. Never have cockroaches been linked to any epidemic of human disease. The roaches themselves tend to stay healthy, both during the six months or less they require to grow to maturity, and for another six to eighteen months of adult life.

Most of the 3,500 different kinds of cockroaches quickly flee from danger and avoid any hideaway that is opened frequently and exposed to light. The Madeira Cockroach (*Leucophaea maderae*), which reached the United States by way of South America and the West Indies, emits a noxious odor if disturbed. A three-inch Madagascan cockroach,

Gromphodorina madagascarensis, hisses loudly by expelling air through a pair of special breathing pores on its sides. The hiss can be heard as far as twelve feet away. The sound is also produced by males courting or battling for territory, and more gently by a female becoming receptive to a mate. So fastidious are the Madagascan roaches that they seem unlikely to invade human quarters. Entomologists have begun keeping them as pets, wondering if anything could be added to their diet to induce them to grow wings. Already well-fed adults of this species develop short, blunt horns, which seem unusual among insects so wont to slither away from confrontation.

Don Marquis, celebrated columnist for the New York *Evening Sun* during the 1920s, made a hero of his office cockroach, archy, who supposedly pecked out poetic whimsy by leaping upon one typewriter key after another whenever Marquis left a blank sheet of paper in his machine. Unable to depress the shift key, archy was constrained to write in lower-case. The lives of archy and mehitabel, the office cat, were familiar delights to many.

Nonetheless, Marquis' readers and others continued to battle every cockroach they found, accustoming these insects to so many poisons that they became immune. This feud between humankind and the indomitable roaches seems unending. Open a long-shut closet in Florida or Mexico and several cockroaches scurry into dark corners. Lift a pile of dead palm fronds outside and "wild" roaches of the identical species clatter away over the dry vegetation. If the fumigator makes the indoors inhospitable, the roaches escape and bide their time, to return when the insecticide has dissipated. After 300 million years in changing environments, these insects are well equipped to survive every challenge while life of any kind can still exist.

89. *With their cylindrical bodies, long threadlike antennae, and a habit of standing motionless for hours on end, the stick insects (family Phasmidae) are renowned masters of protective camouflage. In many species the total loss of wings—hardly needed by insects with such a sedentary and carefree lifestyle—enhances the sticklike imagery. Although stick insects occur as far north as Canada, the majority are found in the tropics. Some Asian species attain a length of more than twelve inches, making them the longest insects in the world. As with leaf insects, parthenogenesis—reproduction without fertilization—commonly occurs. The ratio of female stick insects to males is estimated to be one thousand to one.*
(Michel Casino/Jacana)

90 and **91.** *Patient predators with insatiable appetites—the female is likely to devour the male once they have mated—mantids (family Mantidae) wait in ambush with their large and powerful forelegs folded as if praying for the success of the day's hunt. Spines and teeth on the legs make it impossible for prey to escape, once seized with a lightning-fast strike; large mantids capture not only insects but lizards, frogs, and even small birds. Largest of its kind, the four-inch-long Chinese mantid (Tenodera aridifolia), top left, was introduced in North America in the 1890s to control plant pests. Many mantids are colored and shaped to blend with their environment.*

Photographed in the rainforest of Panama, Choeradodis rhombicollis, top right, has a leaflike expansion of the prothorax that makes this mantid difficult to spot in the mass of green vegetation. And the grizzled mantis (Gonatista grisea), opposite page, disappears among the lichens that blotch the trunk of a bald cypress in a Florida swamp. (90 top left Harry Ellis; top right François Gohier; bottom Belinda Wright; 91 Larry West)

92. *A bordered mantid (Stagmomantis limbata) lurks on a gumweed in a Texas field. Mantids bite the neck of their insect prey, easily piercing the exoskeleton and severing the nerve cord. Their own nervous system is highly decentralized; mantids can lose part of their body and still function, and headless females will lay eggs.* (Robert W. Mitchell)

93. *A West African mantid,* Tarachodes afzelli, *is flattened against her well-camouflaged egg mass, affixed to a twig and protected by a leathery coating called the ootheca. Female mantids produce as many as 350 eggs at a time, covering them with a dense, foamy secretion that quickly hardens and, after several months, will resist even a sharp knife. Mantid eggs are laid in the fall; in spring the ootheca softens and young mantids emerge. Within fifteen minutes their exoskeletons harden and they embark on their first hunt for tiny insects. As they grow larger, they prey on even larger insects.* (Jean Paul Hervy/ Jacana)

94 *overleaf. A South American mantid,* Phyllovates, *strikes a threat posture, displaying the normally hidden red colors of its wings. Mantids are strong fliers, occasionally appearing on the observation decks of towering skyscrapers. And their middle and hind legs are well developed; indeed, some desert species prefer to run down their prey rather than wait in concealment. The natural enemies of mantids include birds, small mammals, and reptiles, but they are fearless insects. Pet mantids have been known to scrap with household cats and dogs.* (François Gohier)

96. *Amidst the heather of an English moor, a Great Green Bush-cricket* (Tettigonia viridissima) *feeds on a bog bush-cricket. Capable of flights exceeding 100 yards, this is one of Europe's best-known insects, and a common chirruping voice on summer nights. This grasshopper munches plants during the early stages of its life, but the adult becomes a hunter—a fairly uncommon habit among orthopterans—preying especially on larvae of the potato beetle. The Great Green Bush-cricket also is noted for its unusually long tegmina—the leathery fore wings that protect its hind flight wings.* (Heather Angel/Biofotos)

Singing Insects

Whether we are in Florida in winter or Alaska in summer, the world feels right when we hear a cricket chirping. All across America this familiar call is a summons to a mate by the common black male Field Cricket (*Gryllus pennsylvanicus*). He has 142 teeth in a filelike array on the undersurface of his right front wing where it overlaps a hard crosswise ridge, or scraper, on the upper surface of his left front wing. As he shrugs his shoulders at high speed, he produces a triple note—sometimes translated as "Please come here!"—at a pitch near the top of the piano's range (4,900 cycles per second).

When a female Field Cricket appears, the male dances around her, stroking her with his antennae; stimulated by her odor, he changes his call to a single pulse at the same frequency. He uses only about sixty-seven of the teeth on his file for his summoning song, raising it from the scraper to separate the beats. His single courtship signal uses about ninety-two teeth in one continuous chirp.

The male European House Cricket, or "Cricket-on-the-Hearth" (*Acheta domestica*), which makes itself at home behind the warm oven in any bakery and can subsist merely on scattered crumbs, has 133 teeth on his file. He also makes a triple chirp until he actually begins courting a specific female. Perhaps she is sensitive to his song, which is slightly lower in pitch than that of the American Field Cricket. The House Cricket reveals his thrill at meeting a potential mate by producing a continuous trill higher than anything possible on the piano, with occasional chirps in the ultrasonic range.

Male crickets are kept as pets in the Orient because of their fighting ability. Their songs escape through the bars of cricket cages, but are appreciated chiefly as signs of continued health. One tiny species, kept as a pet by the Japanese, was known as the *kusa-hibari*, or "grass lark," because of its beautiful and soothing trill. The 19th-century traveler Lafcadio Hearn housed one of these diminutive crickets in a cage only an inch high, and wrote of his sadness when it died because a servant forgot to feed it.

Although we cannot hear the triple chirp of any black cricket as more than a single sound, the interval between one chirp and the next does vary with the air temperature. Chirps come in quick succession on warm nights. On a chilly evening, the intervals grow longer until the cricket stops altogether. The pitch of the chirp changes, too, a fact leading A. E. Dolbear to suggest that anyone with perfect pitch might be able to estimate the temperature from the tone of the cricket's call.

Dolbear discovered that an unknown cricket, which later turned out to be the common Snowy Tree Cricket (*Oecanthus fultoni*) of America, adjusted its chirping rate at a speed he could count. He computed the temperature in degrees Fahrenheit by taking the number of chirps delivered in fifteen seconds and adding forty—thirty chirps at 70°, thirty-five at 75°, forty chirps on a hot 80° night, or ten chirps in fifteen seconds at 50° on a chilly October evening. Actually, at anything much cooler than 60° or warmer than 100°, these crickets usually stop singing altogether. The song of the Snowy Tree Cricket has been well known for centuries. Nathaniel Hawthorne found it so enchanting as to declare, "If moonlight could be heard, it would sound like that."

The Snowy's message differs enough from the calls produced by other male tree crickets that any female of his kind should be able to distinguish it before she approaches him. On a night field trip with our flashlight, we find the male standing motionless, patiently raising his paddle-shaped, pale green wings and fretting file against scraper. Often a calling male will position himself where two broad leaves come together at an angle, creating the effect of a megaphone as the sound projects outward in one direction from between the two leaves. If the sound is directed away from a listener, the call of the tree cricket sounds soft and distant. For this reason tree crickets are often described as ventriloquists. As the cricket's note resonates through those thin, transparent wings, the tree cricket exposes an odorous, pitlike gland high on his back. His call may identify him and dissuade other males of his kind from invading his territory. His fragrant lure induces the female to approach and nibble on the scent gland. While she does so, he swivels imperceptibly and joins his abdomen to hers. She leaves when her eggs have been fertilized.

Continuous calls are the mark of other tree crickets. The Black-horned Tree Cricket (*O. nigricornis*), a half-inch long and pale yellowish-green in hue, pitches his call at the third F above middle C and trills it for fifteen seconds or more. The Four-spotted Tree Cricket (*O. quadripunctatus*) puts out double pulses at B in the second octave above middle C. Each of these singers can and does adjust his pitch slightly to make it match precisely the output of other males of his species within his hearing range. If one male takes alarm and goes silent, his song is continued unchanged by neighbors on adjacent bushes. The silent cricket lowers his wings, saves his scent, and waits a minute or more before resuming his invitations. With the aid of a flashlight, we see the silent females creeping about, their enormously long antennae twitching to investigate everything in reach. They keep their narrower pale green wings wrapped tightly around their bodies; their long, slender legs are poised for a sudden leap into the night if any danger threatens.

In almost any land, the crickets and grasshoppers and katydids offer the summer season's last symphony orchestra. Their songs ring through the air of autumn, each musician following his own tune. Large katydids, with their broader wings, stridulate their messages through the dark hours from shrub or tree. By day, the slimmer meadow grasshoppers cling to weeds in the pasture and flit nervously ahead of us as we walk along. Both of these insects, long-horned grasshoppers of the family Tettigoniidae, have antennae longer than their bodies and overlap the left wing over the right, instead of right over left like any cricket of the family Gryllidae.

Jean Henri Fabre interpreted the autumn music as the insects' method "of expressing the joy of living, the universal joy which every animal species celebrates after its kind." Perhaps Hal Borland was more realistic about the hum and buzz and scratch we hear when he said, ". . . summer is a lifetime to a katydid—birth and growth and maturity, which ends in old age and death . . . the urgency of time is now upon the insect world."

The male of the so-called True Katydid (*Pterophylla camellifolia*) seems to get into an argument with himself, switching from his emphatic three-pulsed "Kay-tee-Did!" to his four-pulsed negative "Kay-tee-Did-n't!" His first pulse is invariably the briefest, and the subsequent ones are progressively longer because each additional fret of teeth against scraper makes his wing resonate more strongly, close to D in the highest octave on the piano. We have no way to tell which is the "call" and which the "answer," unless the second comes from another katydid responding to the first. They do alternate when males are establishing territories in a tree, where they will stand and call until a female arrives. The insect's call indicates sexual readiness. It fades away as soon as a male has mated. If he is still vigorous, he may mate again the following night; meanwhile, his tree is available to any other katydid that wants it.

Seated in the sun among the weeds of an open field, we can watch a Slender Meadow Grasshopper (*Conocephalus fasciatus*) make his music. He twitches his wings to produce a series of faint practice notes, *tip, tip, tip*, then buzzes forth a *tse-e-e-e* lasting from five to twenty seconds. His is the softest love song we hear, one which may persist at intervals day or night. Success at attracting a mate must come often enough in darkness to compensate the species for the number of males an owl will locate and devour. Later, at its roost, the bird will regurgitate the indigestible head capsules of the Slender Meadow Grasshopper.

Far more vigorous calls come from the American Shield-bearer (*Atlanticus americanus*), which buzzes a continuous train of pulses despite the fact that his overlapping front wings are so short as to be scarcely visible from above. With such abbreviated equipment, he cannot fly.

While we watch the long-horned grasshoppers in sunlight, several short-horned locusts (Locustidae) distract us. They rattle out their sounds by rubbing together a scraper or row of peglike teeth on the inner surface of the hind thighs and a row of teeth or a scraper along a vein of the wing cover. The effect may be no more musical than that of a fingernail scraped along the tips of the teeth of a pocket comb. Short-horns listen for these sounds with ears on each side of the first abdominal segment. Flush with the surface of the body, the eardrum appears huge by comparison with the neat oval membranes that cover the ears of katydids and crickets; in the latter two, the ears are situated just beyond the knee joint on each front leg.

Most famous and widely dispersed of the short-horns is the Migratory Locust (*Locusta migratoria*) of Africa and the Near East. Five different varieties inhabit the great grasslands of Africa, Eurasia south of the spruce-fir forests, parts of the East Indies, and tropical Australia. They range as far as New Zealand. Those that arrived like a devastating tornado in Egypt as the "Eighth Plague" predicted by Moses must have been no less fearsome than earlier and subsequent swarms. Until 1921, the phenomenon defied understanding. Then the Migratory Locust was found to be sluggish in any country so long as its numbers remained small. In normal dry years, the lack of water keeps most grasshopper eggs from hatching. The few nymphs that emerge have little opportunity to see one another, let alone compete for scarce food. Then a few rainy years in succession let more eggs hatch, and more young are stimulated to competition. Their color changes and the body grows broader, with bigger intestinal muscles. Any local shortage of food starts the young locusts marching; at first just a few, then increasing numbers of the insects, set out in search of nourishment, eating everything they can find. One final molt gives them wings and lets the swarm take off into whatever wind is blowing across open land.

The pilot of a jet airplane drew our attention to one huge swarm below us as he postponed his descent toward a landing at Addis Ababa, Ethiopia. A few high-flying locusts had already splashed against the windshield of the cockpit at 20,000 feet. The rest flew much lower, in great rust-brown clouds, each swarm composed of hundreds of tons of insects. We could imagine the continuous roar of so many wings, without having to share the dismay of people on the ground where locusts settle to refuel. Reputedly, one ton of these insects consumes daily as much food as ten elephants, twenty-five camels, or 250 people.

Wherever they settle, locusts strip the vegetation clean. No longer are the swarms followed by great flocks of European white storks wintering in Africa and eating every locust they can catch. Man-made changes in the environment at the northern and southern ends of the storks' migration route have changed the world for storks, and thus for plague locusts as well.

Some of the world's locusts lack both file and scraper, yet still identify themselves with a distinctive sound. The common Carolina Locust (*Dissosteira carolina*) of North America is silent on the ground. The male leaps into a display flight, showing off the yellow border around his black hind wings while snapping the narrow front pair against the hind pair. The crackling sound, usually composed of about twelve clicks per second, persists while the insect hovers over something of interest on the ground—perhaps a female that the male sees and we do not. On occasion, a Carolina Locust will become alarmed and precede us down some path as though he were a butterfly, snapping his wings sporadically, perhaps as a warning to other males.

A relative of the Carolina Locust, the Cracker Grasshopper (*Circotettix verruculatus*), lives on the bare rocky summits of mountains in New England. The loud crackling noise it produces during its display flight has given this grasshopper its common name. Sometimes a displaying male will hover in front of a cliff, and the crackling sound is amplified as it bounces off the rock. The sulphur-winged grasshoppers (*Arphia*) have a softer call, but they are conspicuous as they hover over dry fields and hilltops in eastern North America, their bright yellow wings flashing in the sunlight.

On distant continents, neither short-horned nor long-horned grasshoppers have impressed us with their sounds. The British Short-horn (*Psophus stridulus*) makes a loud clapping sound as it takes wing, but is silent as soon as it is airborne. In this it reminds us of a startled pigeon or a dove that smacks its wings together above its back for the first few beats as it struggles to gain altitude.

In England and on the Continent, the Great Green Bush-cricket (*Tettigonia viridissima*), a long-horn with a wingspan of almost two inches, calls *zick-zick* in late autumn from some high bush or low tree where a female might pay attention. The Oak Bush-cricket

(*Meconema thalassinum*), a slender, pale green European species, has no sound-producing organs; instead the males beat their legs on leaves, making a soft, rattling sound. The Wart-biter (*Decticus verrucivorus*), a sturdy green and yellow insect with long green antennae, provides a similar summons all over Europe. This unfortunate locust is the subject of a popular legend, and is often caught by children who believe that the brown juice from the insect's mouth will remove warts.

Allen Keast tells of no special sound from the forty-five different leaping grasshoppers, crickets, and katydids that have colonized Hawaii. We heard nothing from the lively big Bird Locusts (*Schistocerca melanocera*) that leaped and flitted over the lava fields on the Galápagos Islands. Most of the few other grasshoppers on the Galápagos are wingless and inconspicuous; whether they have songs to sing remains a mystery.

Ears on the front legs or body, pegs on the hind thighs, and file and scraper on overlapping areas of wings are all preserved in the fossil record, proving that the ancestors of grasshoppers, katydids, and crickets were putting their own sounds to vital use long before the world had any frog or toad to croak, or bird to sing, or mammal to roar. Almost always, it was a male producing a distinctive note that invited a female of his kind to approach. These one-way conversations clearly began on Earth among the leaping members of one insect order. Only later did cicadas take up the practice, in their own way, and become the noisiest of all. The whine of a mosquito, the squeak of a beetle, and the buzz of a bee, all came much later.

Aristotle was thoroughly familiar with these insect singers, but he disqualified all of them from any claim to a voice since they lacked his two requirements: tongue and lung. We can only regret that Aristotle had no chance to experience the sounds at the edge of a great rainforest in the tropics. There, time follows a special rhythm. The tick of the clock is the call of birds, of frogs and toads, of katydids. It is the whine of cicadas, the patter of feet on leaves, the pelt of downpouring rain. As we heard it on a July evening, by six o'clock in the gathering darkness from the colonnade of tree trunks came an occasional whine, a long, steady buzz that might deepen as though to run down, then rise again. The note would coast almost to a stop, pick up sharply, coast once more, and finally die altogether. Within minutes, the combined sounds had become almost deafening. Yet by 6:50 the katydids were replacing the cicadas, filling the silences with clicks and buzzes from the shrubby undergrowth in the clearing and from every level in the trees. They had the whole night to attract a mate, while the cicadas took their rest.

Today we can record for replay and analysis the sounds these leaping insects produce and we can even investigate the mechanism of their inheritance. Using the technique of artificial insemination, we can overcome the unwillingness of a female to respond to a male of a related species whose call is not the summons she should heed. Will the hybrids make sounds like the male parent or the mother, or will they attract the attention of unmodified adults of either species? We could use our technology to anticipate what new features a cricket might introduce into its chirp and, from sympathetic members of its audience, isolate the beginnings of a new and distinctive species. We are unwilling to believe that every winning combination is already with us. The challenge for us is to recognize, among the age-old symphonies the insects conduct, the modern music that also has a future.

If our ears are sharp and our memories clear, we might recognize a different sound in a familiar place. Experience tells us that this may mean that cricket or grasshopper from some distant land has arrived in our midst as a potential colonist. After all, no one in America heard a House Cricket until this insect managed to ride some boat from Europe. Now we can learn how females of this engaging species space out their territories indoors, unwittingly reserving for their close kin the local supply of food. Male House Crickets also establish their territories in audible ways that are meaningful to members of their own sex and less so to females. A female risks involvement in a brawl if she invades the odorous environs of another female. But she gains acceptance on her own merits if she ignores the warning sound with which a male of her species keeps other males at a distance. *Vive la différence!*

105. *A short-horned grasshopper nymph (family Acrididae) poses on a Black-eyed Susan in a Michigan meadow. Among grasshoppers, locusts, katydids, and crickets, metamorphosis is relatively simple. Newly hatched nymphs resemble the adults, but are much smaller and lack developed wings and sex organs. As many as ten molts occur during maturation, although four to six is the normal number.* (John Shaw)

106 *overleaf. Until the final molt, the position of the wings of this short-horned grasshopper nymph (family Acrididae) will be reversed. That is, the small, flaplike hind wings rest atop the tegmina. Orthopterans generally produce one generation a year, embryonic development taking several months. Many species produce their eggs in autumn, the nymphs emerging in the spring. The female short-horned grasshopper scratches out a hole in the dirt with her ovipositor, depositing up to two dozen fertilized eggs and covering them with a waterproof secretion. Each female may produce several egg masses.* (Jack Drafahl/ Kritter Labs)

108 *top left. In the eucalypt forest near Darwin, an Australian grasshopper (Valanga sp.) has shed its nymphal skin for the final time and is drying its fully developed wings. There are some 23,000 species of orthopterans worldwide, ranging in size from pygmy locusts half an inch long to a giant New Zealand grasshopper measuring fourteen inches from the tip of its antennae to the ends of its hind legs. (Stanley Breeden)*

108 *bottom left. A Speckled Sand Grasshopper (Trimerotropis helferi) in its final nymphal stage is nearly invisible on a California dune. This species frequents the dry sand zone on ocean beaches and adjacent dunes. It is one of the band-winged grasshoppers (subfamily Oedipodinae) found in arid environments. Their crackling noise and the lively color of the hind wings make them conspicuous in flight. But when they alight with their hind wings concealed, they vanish into the background. (Thomas W. Davies)*

108 *top center. The common name of the Lubber Grasshopper (Brachystola magna) of the western United States means big and clumsy. It is an apt description for a three-inch insect that can hardly flutter, let alone fly, because of its small hind wings. Indeed, great swarms of Lubber Grasshoppers can be seen marching across highways until the pavement becomes treacherously slick from their squashed bodies. The Lubber's foul smell is protection against enemies. (C. Allan Morgan)*

108 *bottom center. The bold, blue-black bands of the Three-banded Grasshopper (Hadrotettix trifasciatus) serve to break up the insect's outline. Note that bands on the fore wing align with markings on the hind femur. This handsome species inhabits rangeland from Canada to Texas, feeding on grass and herbaceous foliage.* (Robert W. Mitchell)

109 *top right. The strange appearance of the hooded grasshopper (family Acrididae), found in the bamboo forests of India, is due to unusual development of the pronotum and great lateral compression of the body. Grasshoppers eat with their agile front legs; the middle legs provide support; and the powerful hind legs are adapted for jumping, with sharp spines that dig into the ground and provide traction like a runner's spiked shoes.* (Stanley Breeden)

109 *bottom right. Rubbing the rough surface of its hind wings against the fore wings, a Short-horned Grasshopper (Hippiscus ocetate) sends its song—a low buzz —into the Texas desert night. One writer with colorful accuracy has referred to the grasshopper's head as resembling "a medieval jousting horse outfitted for battle."* (Robert W. Mitchell)

110 *overleaf. In the tropical forest of Borneo, a katydid (family Tettigoniidae) stands on its head in a defensive posture, revealing bright colors that a predator may associate with nauseating smell or taste. But the katydid's best protection is the kick of its powerful hind legs.* (Kjell B. Sandved)

112. *A Cone-headed Grasshopper (Neoconocephalus robusta) climbs a paper birch tree in Michigan to feed on the foliage. As one might suspect from the sharklike profile, Cone-heads can give a nasty bite if seized by a predator. The conventional grasshopper reaction is to spit up harmless brown saliva. Female Cone-heads and katydids use bladelike ovipositors to cut slits in plant stems, depositing their eggs in the soft tissue. (Robert P. Carr)*

113 *top left. At dawn in a Queensland eucalypt forest, a long-horned grasshopper (family Tettigoniidae) hangs from its last nymphal skin. Its wings expand as blood circulates to the veins, helped by the pull of gravity in the upside-down position. (Stanley Breeden)*

113 *top right. An immature female bush katydid (Scudderia sp.) rests on the bud of a cardinal-flower in a Connecticut nature preserve. Named for their shrill and ceaseless song, these bright green grasshoppers are a common voice of the night in late summer and early autumn. The male katydid is the vocalist, its song serving as a mating serenade and a warning to enemies. Katydids hear by means of tympana, membranes that resemble a human ear, that are attached to their front legs. (Robert L. Carissimi)*

113 *bottom. This unusually colorful long-horned grasshopper (family Tettigoniidae) was photographed in a rainforest in India. Long-horned grasshoppers are named for their extraordinarily long antennae. To specialists, the songs of many grasshoppers and katydids are as distinctive as bird songs, recognizable by the number, pitch, and sequence of the notes. (Stanley Breeden)*

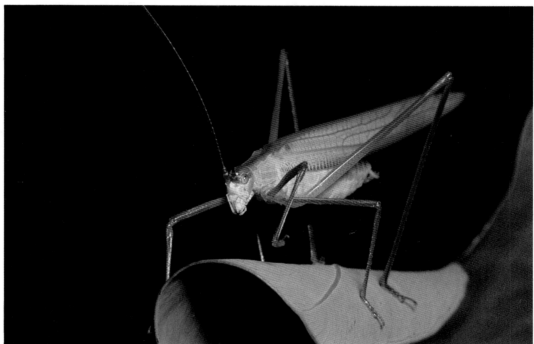

114 *overleaf. Evolution has left this European Katydid (Barbistes serricauda) wingless except for the vestigial, orange-brown fore wings, or tegmina, which are its sound-producing instruments.*
(Heiko Bellmann/Bildarchiv Jürgen Lindenburger)

116. *The tiny first-stage nymph of a katydid,* Leptophyes punctatissima, *is poised on the stem of a fallen leaf. While tropical species may live as long as a year, in cool northern regions orthopterans die with the first frost, having left countless billions of eggs to repopulate fields and forests the following spring.* (Patrick Lorne/Jacana)

117 *top. A stick grasshopper,* Apioscelis bulbosa, *from Peru has close-set eyes and antennae concentrated on a narrow dorsal extension of its head. Stick grasshoppers of the family* Prosopidae *are native to South America. They are wingless, mute, and deaf, with long, thin hind legs that are of little use for jumping. Like stick insects, they escape the attention of predators by resembling twigs.* (Edward S. Ross)

117 *bottom. Two and a half inches long, a Long-headed Toothpick Grasshopper (*Radinonatum brevipenne*) hides on a twig in Florida's Ocala National Forest. One of the more unusual grasshoppers in North America, this species is found mainly in Gulf Coast states. Its odd shape serves it well as camouflage, especially when it perches on a brown stem or blade of grass, with its legs and antennae pressed against the plant.* (John Shaw)

118 *overleaf. Eumastacids are peculiar tropical grasshoppers, found mostly in the New World, that live in foliage rather than on the ground. In their characteristic pose, they rest with hind legs outspread and make no effort to conceal their bright colors. The red genitalia of this wingless male is an added warning signal to predators that the eumastacid makes an unsavory meal.* (Edward S. Ross)

120. *The wing scales of a Mourning Cloak* (Nymphalis antiopa), *greatly magnified. The dark, iridescent wings of this familiar butterfly are bordered by a band of creamy yellow and a row of brilliant blue spots. The Mourning Cloak is one of the first butterflies to be seen in spring, for the last brood of autumn hibernates, often emerging before the snow has fully melted. The Mourning Cloak is common in the New World, where it is found from Alaska and subarctic Canada discontinuously to Venezuela. In England, where it is a rare stray from continental Europe, collectors prize it as the "Camberwell Beauty."* (John Shaw)

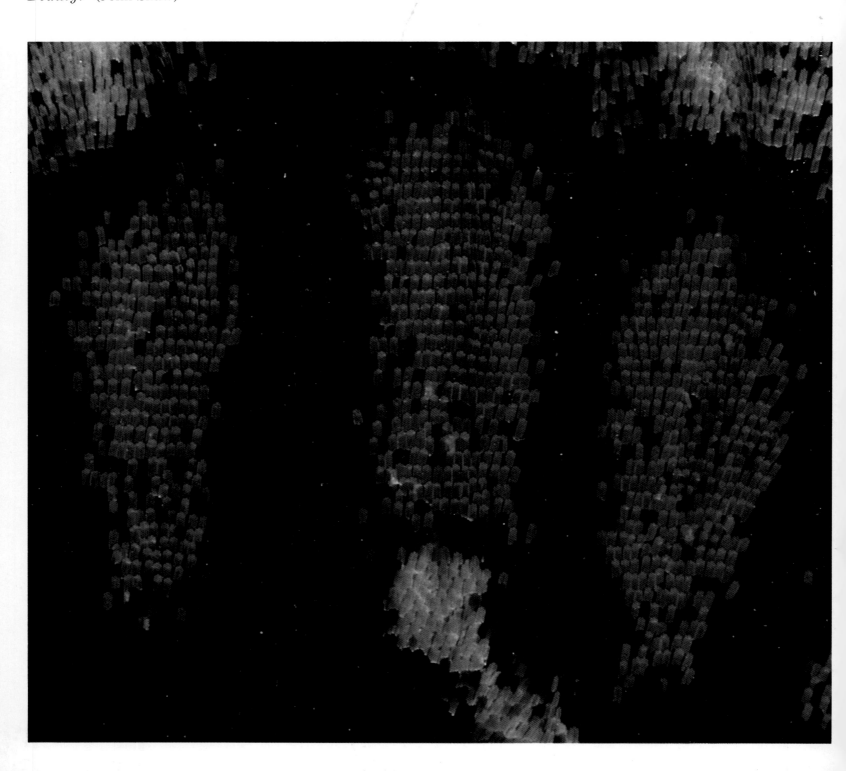

Designs Aloft

Just how free is a butterfly? Without restraint it fans
its bright wings while probing with a long, uncoiled
tongue deep into the secret nectaries of a summer
flower. Each blossom is a way station along a
seemingly erratic route, a potential trysting place, as
well as a source of water and energy to fuel the
animal's travel. The insect actually follows a pattern
of inherited instructions—a whole "parliament of
instincts"—as it responds to stimuli from within and
outside its body. Like a ballerina or a circus clown, it
gives the impression of effortless, aimless movement,
but we know a butterfly has a mission to perform, a
mate to meet, a posterity to ensure.

No cabbage patch in America is too small or isolated
to attract a Cabbage White (*Pieris rapae*). This
butterfly was introduced accidentally from Europe to
Quebec in 1860 and to New York in 1868. It needed
only twenty years to spread across half the United
States and Canada, and today, between spring and
fall in just about any garden, we are likely to see a
white male with only a few dark spots on his fore
wings. He rises and falls among the tall plants,
settling on none, stopping only for an occasional sip of
nectar. Every small patch of white rates a closer
look, but none is distinct to him at a distance greater
than a foot. At a distance, the male may mistake a
white daisy for a female. Suddenly his antennae pick
up an attractive scent. He alights an inch away from
something white and turns his antennae, spread like
a V, toward it. It is a female Cabbage White; she
opens and closes her wings above her back, her
perfume sending an unmistakable invitation to him.

The courtship gestures of the Grayling Butterfly (*Satyrus semele*) in Eurasia are more elaborate, and they intrigued Professor Niko Tinbergen, now of Oxford University. He recorded their antics in his native Holland, where female Graylings wear an extra eyespot conspicuously on their fore wings and the male has a small brown dot at the corresponding location on his equally tawny wings. We have seen butterflies of this kind on the stony shores of Öland, off the Swedish coast of the Baltic Sea. Gusty winds interfered with the insects' interaction but did not upset the sequence. Tinbergen noted a progression in the repartee of alternating gestures that lead to the male's learning whether the female is receptive to his advances. After he has alighted near by, she has only to walk away from him, flapping her wings vigorously, to tell him "No!" in a language he understands; she is announcing that she is already mated and in no need of attention. A female without a mate, on the other hand, will sit still, letting the male walk around her and make the next move. Without this encouragement, he may as well find a new post on a stone or shrub and wait for the next flier to come along. He may end up pursuing a butterfly of another kind, a wasp, grasshopper, dragonfly, dung beetle, or even his own shadow. The suitability of his choice will become apparent only after he has approached his target.

A male Grayling, like many other butterflies, can be attracted to a paper decoy of the right size fluttering at the end of a string. A male Cabbage White will do his best to keep up, although his powers of flight are more feeble. A Red Admiral (*Vanessa atalanta*) may not clearly distinguish the details of the paper model, but will give it attention if it flashes an orange or red stripe like that on his own fore wings. Any crayon mark will do if the hue is close to that of the insect. The color means nothing to a Cabbage or Grayling, which lack such decorations.

Our excellent eyes allow us to inspect a butterfly in finer detail than any potential mate could manage, but our noses fail to inform us of the exquisite differences between individuals. We see that no two are quite alike in pattern, although a general scheme of colors, scallops, and spots is amply evident. Hue and design appeal to us as the badge of butterfly kind, the stimuli for artist and poet; yet the caterpillars from one butterfly mother, fed a uniform diet appropriate to their species, do not mature as faithful copies of the parent or of any other in the brood. Identical human twins often reveal far more similarity.

Variation in both wing shape and coloration becomes extreme in the Mocker Butterfly (*Papilio dardanus*) of Africa. Except in Ethiopia and Madagascar, where its heritage is revealed by tails on the hind wings, it is a "tail-less swallowtail." On Madagascar, both male and female are large and cream-colored, with black borders and black tails. Elsewhere, the females occur in more than a dozen color forms. Coloration ranges from almost totally black to black and white, black and orange, black and yellow, and orange and white. Mockers vary so greatly that for years they were assumed to be different species.

Failure by a swallowtail to develop tails might be dangerous. This feature has long been believed to be an expendable target, a distraction for butterfly-catching birds. If a bird seizes one of the tails in its beak, the tail tears loose and the butterfly escapes. Yet the lack of tails in a Mocker helps the insect to resemble distasteful butterflies of quite different kinds—not just one or two, but at least fourteen across the African continent. Several different forms of Mocker can live together in the same forest canopy without predators discovering which ones are edible. In most of their sampling, the predators catch the more numerous unpalatable kinds. Only a male Mocker has the need to discriminate between those with which he can mate and those that are too unlike him. On the islands in Lake Victoria, the males must be in special need of scent cues and signals, for there the variable female Mockers run riot in distinctive colors and patterns.

In the eastern United States, the widespread Tiger Swallowtail (*Papilio glaucus*) has two types of females in the Southeast but only one elsewhere. In areas where the unpalatable Pipevine Swallowtail (*Battus philenor*) is common, dark-phase Tiger females abound, and the paler ones that resemble the males are scarce. Observation reveals that the males prefer to pursue females like themselves, with straw-colored wings narrowly striped with black. But although more acceptable to the male, the pale Tiger female of the Southeast is more susceptible prey; many such females, after mating, are caught by birds before they can lay all their eggs. Dark Tigers—

brownish-black with orange spots near the wing margins, like those on a Pipevine Swallowtail—are common; their resemblance to the Pipevine keeps them safe, and the color phase is perpetuated because birds tend to avoid them.

The American tropics have whole families of inedible butterflies; the heliconians (Heliconiidae) are the most conspicuous. With long, slender bodies and long, rounded wings, they quiver through the tropical forest clearings with no sign of haste. A familiar outlier is the Zebra Butterfly (*Heliconius charitonius*) of southernmost Florida, the West Indies, and the more southern New World tropics, which gets its name from the narrow lemon-yellow stripes on its black wings. After sunset, some of these butterflies flew past us through the fading light to a favorite bare branch, there to settle for the night. Dozens assembled at the site and found acceptable spots between familiar neighbors. Silently, but with gentle jostling, each gained its special perch for the slumber party, and maintained its place in the group until after sunrise. Probably the combined odor of the little throng would repel a predator more than any single sleeping heliconian could. But each of these butterflies has another trick to extend its life. It gathers pollen from a flower, wets it with nectar and permits digestion among its mouthparts to release amino acids in solution—an elixir that keeps the butterfly's reproductive system renewed for months instead of the usual few weeks of adult butterfly activity. Each heliconian extends its opportunity to teach a butterfly-eater—whether bird, lizard, or monkey—that insects with their color pattern should be left alone.

The colors of a heliconian are pigments within the individual scales on the transparent membrane of its wings. Each scale is of a single color but has a definite place in the mosaic that determines the butterfly's appearance. High above the heliconians in the rainforest fly the *Morphos*, large butterflies with no pigment at all, yet their broad wings reflect the sunlight like mirrors of iridescent blue. The hue is an interference color, as magical as the spectrum from a colorless diamond or a raindrop. It arises where light is turned back along its course from thin transparent layers in the scale, concentrating much of the energy into a single wavelength.

The spectacular *Morpho* butterflies display their

magnificence by coasting and flapping infrequently, unless two males fly close together and begin a duel for dominance. The less brightly colored females reveal themselves less often, spending their time in the forest shadows. It is almost exclusively the males that provide the blue flashes we can see above the forest from a low-flying airplane. The *Morphos* enchanted us in Suriname by flying, now low, now high, above the jungle river as we progessed in a dugout canoe. Females of the species met us along forest paths in dense shade, where they stopped occasionally for the intoxicating flavor of rotting fruit or some nutrient-rich sap dripping from a wounded tree. The largest of the South American beauties, *Morpho hecuba*, has a wingspan of about eight inches, and so intricate a pattern of brown spots beneath its wings that it can disappear instantly into the uncertain forest shadows by settling and drawing together its wings above its back.

So gaudy are these flashing *Morphos* that in the past they were often collected and used for jewelry. Enthusiasts used to build flimsy ladders into the forest canopy, and, climbing high into the branches, reach out with a long-handled net to capture an iridescent butterfly. Brazil now has a law forbidding the capture of butterflies for jewelry; most trade comes from insects raised in captivity.

In Papua New Guinea, too, the practice of raising butterflies is spreading. Native people find the caterpillars of particular kinds and feed them an appropriate diet in order to raise perfect butterflies for export to meet the world's demand. The wonderful birdwing butterflies (*Ornithoptera* spp.), once collected in large numbers wherever a group of them assembled at a mud-puddle "watering place," can now be obtained without much danger to their wild populations. In some species of birdwings, a collar of brilliant red sets off the wings from the black head and antennae. The color of a single species may vary from island to island in the South Pacific and north to the Philippines. Females tend to be duller and larger; some have a wingspan of ten inches and are the largest of all butterflies.

No one can really doubt that tropical butterflies outrank in size and vividness those of the more temperate lands. Yet far from the Equator, some demand attention for other qualities. We recall the Phoebus Parnassians (*Parnassius phoebus*) that we showed to the poet Mark Van Doren far above timberline in Rocky Mountain National Park. On the high tundra, where harsh climate favors the sedges, grasses, and "cushion plants" between the lichen-coated rocks, Parnassians make short flights on those rare days when the bitter wind subsides and the sun shines warmly. Each has rounded wings the texture and color of parchment, translucent in many areas, dotted here and there with scarlet or black. Their caterpillars stay out of sight, below the tops of the cushion plants, where the solar heat persists for a time and keeps the foliage unfrozen and edible. The caterpillar eats and grows until, often after two years or more, it can transform into an adult. Parnassians have representatives near mountain peaks in Europe, Asia, and western North America; their ancestors managed to spread across the northern hemisphere over the Siberian-Alaskan land bridge. Today's populations inspire poetry in climbers who reach an alpine meadow on almost any pleasant day. In the Himalayas, the Parnassians range to approximately 20,000 feet.

New England peaks are home to mountain butterflies of especially limited range. Suitably nicknamed the arctics (*Oeneis* spp.), they appear to be relicts from the Ice Age, still finding tolerable climate and food plants in the most inhospitable situations. An annual census of the White Mountain Butterfly (*Oeneis semidea*) is held atop Mount Washington, New Hampshire, on a warm spring day when this smoky-brown insect can fly freely. It seems to be holding its own today, nourished as a caterpillar among sedges high above the treeline.

What person admiring the butterflies flitting across a meadow on a summer day can imagine all the contributions from the environment that make these insects possible? We may regard ourselves as being well informed if we can distinguish the butterflies, or know that a skipper (Hesperiidae) is different because it has a curved tip to each antenna instead of a compact club. Most skippers rest with their fore wings not quite pressed together and their hind wings drooping, sometimes lowered against a supporting leaf. In South America, there are more species of skippers than butterflies of other families. This knowledge makes us marvel at the Checkered Skipper (*Pyrgus centaureae*), a circumpolar member of the Arctic butterfly fauna. This skipper is small and dark in eastern North America, where it ranges south to the mountains of Virginia. But in the West it is larger and paler and strictly alpine; there, it is known best from Long's Peak, Colorado, far above timberline.

An impressive range is easy to explain for certain butterflies, since they travel extensively in some years. The Painted Lady (*Vanessa cardui*), so well known and admired in Europe and North America, has a winter brood in North Africa and eastward to Pakistan. On many a spring day, these butterflies swarm northward, cross the Mediterranean Sea, and fly through the high passes of the Alps. By the end of May they are common in southern England and Wales, and a few have passed the Arctic Circle in Scandinavia. In all of these places their caterpillars find a bonanza of thistles and other composites. A mild summer allows countless millions of Painted Ladies to mature and fly south to their winter havens. No wonder this species is sometimes called the "Cosmopolitan." It is found throughout Africa, Asia, Europe, and on many islands. It disappears each year in places where frosts are normal, only to return in another warm season.

The most accomplished traveler in North America is unquestionably the sturdy Monarch (*Danaus plexippus*). English-speaking Canadians call it the "King Billy" because its orange and black markings resemble the heraldic colors of William of Orange, later William III of England. Each autumn, vast numbers wing southward from southern Canada and the northern United States to Florida, the Gulf States, California, and Mexico. Hordes find roosting places on evergreen trees, from which a few venture forth to drink dew and nectar. Until a few years ago, the main destination in Mexico was a mystery. Now Monarchs that have been given distinctive numbered wing tags as far north as Ontario and Minnesota are known to winter in certain areas; those from the Far West spend the cold months at Pacific Grove on California's Monterey Peninsula.

From all of these wintering sites the mated females head north again each spring, arriving where young milkweed plants have grown to a size suitable for eggs and caterpillars. The new brood that matures heads farther north to establish another generation. The process repeats itself, and the butterflies reach all the way to Hudson Bay before the end of summer.

Then, maturing Monarchs head south and complete their trip in a few short weeks. One Monarch tagged on the north shore of Lake Ontario on September 18 was recovered on January 25 at San Luis Potosi, Mexico. This is a straight-line distance of about 1,870 miles, but even with a tailwind the airborne insect's journey would have been much longer. Another Monarch tagged on the same day at the identical place reached Roxie, Mississippi, on October 5, having traveled at least 1,060 miles in the space of seventeen days.

A Monarch might break its voyage on a ship far out to sea, and after a brief rest fly on again. Every night would seem to call for a stop, yet Monarchs reached Britain from North America without known help in 1876, and 214 more were caught there between that year and 1962—as many as 30 were found in some years. Not until later were milkweed plants introduced to Britain, giving the immigrant females a chance to raise a brood.

Monarchs colonized Hawaii in 1845, the Marquesas in 1860, New Caledonia and the east coast of Australia in 1870, and New Zealand four years later. Aptly known in these places as the Wanderer, the Monarch has spread to the East Indies, Malaya, and Burma. Its caterpillars thrive wherever their food plant is well established. Monarch relatives (*Danaus* spp.) inhabit the West Indies and South America. These species have fewer white spots on their wings and show no urge to travel—they may be descendants of Monarchs that settled down.

A butterfly may appear flimsy and flighty, aimless in its aerial antics, but there is meaning and design in its nature, its scaly covering, and its inherited behavior. We deceive ourselves if we interpret its graceful charm in any other way.

129. *Nearly invisible against a vine leaf in a forest clearing is the bristly caterpillar of* Moduza procris, *known as the Commander, a common species in India, Sri Lanka, Bangladesh, and Burma. Commander larvae feed on the foliage of mussaenda, a vine with yellow and white flowers that is grown in greenhouses in the United States. Up to a dozen caterpillars may be found on a single plant.* (Stanley Breeden)

130 *overleaf. The caterpillar of a Tiger Swallowtail (Papilio glaucus) nibbles a wild cherry leaf at the edge of a North Carolina woods. Young larvae of this conspicuous butterfly are brown and white and look like bird droppings. The mature caterpillar is two inches long, bright green, with a pair of startling eyes on its swollen "head" to deter enemies. For shelter, the caterpillar folds the edges of a leaf around its body like a blanket.* (Harry Ellis)

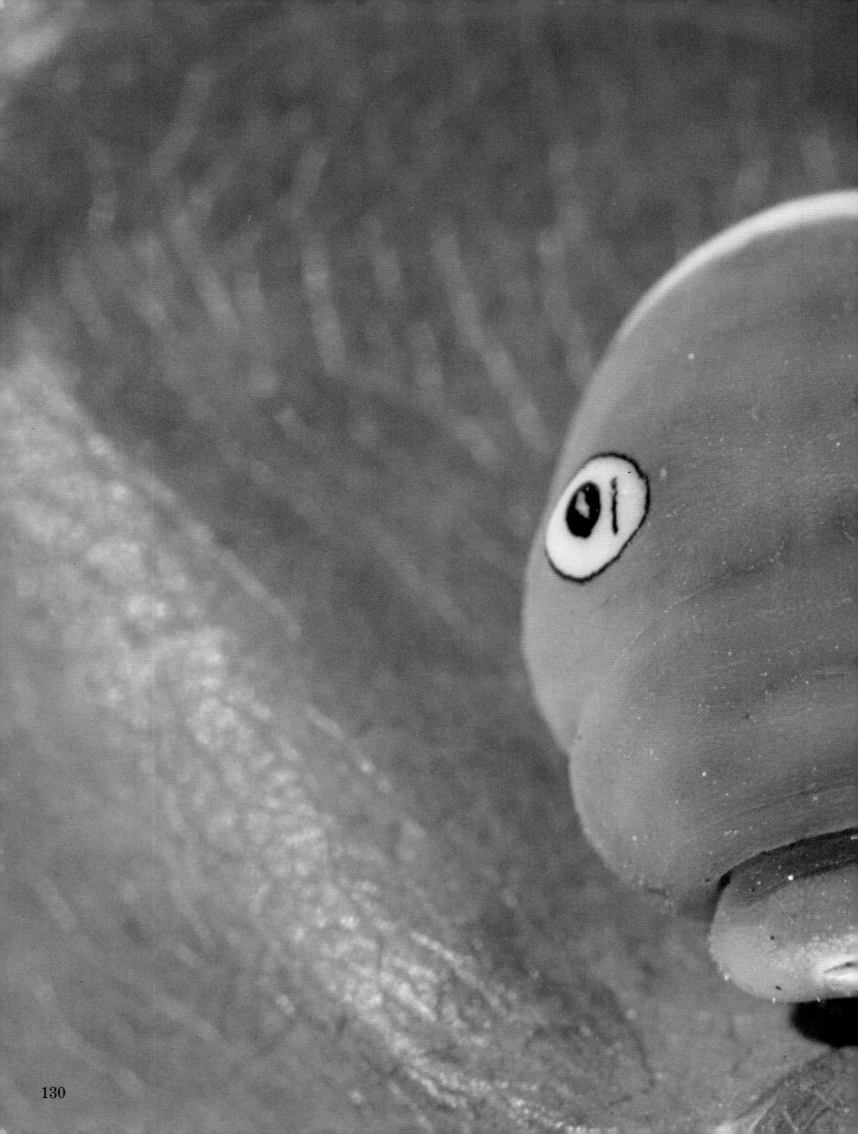

132. *Tiger Swallowtails* (Papilio glaucus) *congregate near a stream in the Tennessee mountains. Scientists have yet to fully explain why some butterflies swarm by the dozens or hundreds at mud puddles, drinking moisture for hours, although researchers recently learned that Tiger Swallowtails extract dissolved sodium salts from the water. Manure heaps and rotting carrion also lure great clusters of butterflies and may supply the insects with essential protein and minerals.* (Sonja Bullaty)

133 *top. The only swallowtail with a circumpolar distribution,* Papilio machaon *is simply called "the Swallowtail" in England, for there it is the only representative of its kind. In North America, where it ranges from the Arctic Ocean south to Lake Superior, the species is known as the Old World Swallowtail. This is one of the best known butterflies in Europe, where its caterpillars feed on cultivated and wild plants of the carrot family; but little is known of its biology in Alaska and Canada.* (Patrick Lorne/Jacana)

133 *bottom. The Eastern Black Swallowtail* (Papilio polyxenes) *drifts like a wind-blown leaf over summer meadows east of the Rocky Mountains, pausing to sip nectar from wildflowers such as this hawkweed. Its caterpillars often can be found feeding on Queen Anne's lace, and they can be troublesome pests in gardens and truck farms, devouring the foliage of carrots, celery, parsley, and dill. There are two or more broods of Eastern Black Swallowtails each summer; the last pupate over winter in a woody chrysalis, emerging in early spring.* (Rod Planck/National Audubon Society Collection/Photo Researchers, Inc.)

134 *overleaf. A Tiger Swallowtail* (Papilio glaucus) *drinks nectar from a wood lily in a northern Michigan forest. Ranging from Alaska to the Gulf Coast, this handsome butterfly is found in a variety of habitats— open woodlands, orchards, gardens, and parks, and along weedy roadsides and riverbanks.* (Rod Planck)

136 top. Few butterflies match the spectacular beauty of the Blue Mountain Swallowtail (Papilio ulysses), found in lowland rainforests in New Guinea, northern Queensland, and the Solomon Islands. Fluttering through the jungle, it flashes its wings like the blue lights of a police car. The Blue Mountain Swallowtail can be easily lured to blue objects placed at the edges of clearings. The larvae feed on the leaves of citrus and related plants. (Thomas W. Davies)

136 center. Although both male and female Tiger Swallowtails (Papilio glaucus) are typically yellow with black stripes across their wings, the females are dimorphic; in the southern United States as many as 95 percent of their sex will be black with a wing border of yellow, blue, and orange spots. This dark form female mimics the Pipevine Swallowtail (Battus philenor), whose adults and caterpillars are distasteful to predators because their host plant, pipevine, contains poisonous chemicals. (Harry Ellis)

136 *bottom. Mating Cairns'*
Birdwings (Ornithoptera priamus
cairnsii) *in the wilds of Queensland.*
Note the difference in size and color
between the male (top) and female.
This species is divided into more
than a dozen geographic races,
based on variations in color. The
bold patterns and hues of birdwings
warn predators of their noxious
taste, for the caterpillars of these
tropical butterflies—like those of
some swallowtails—feed on toxic
plants. Australian law and an
international trade convention
protect birdwings from commercial
exploitation. (Belinda Wright)

137. *Largest of all butterflies are*
the incredibly lovely birdwings of
the genus Ornithoptera, *from*
Southeast Asia, New Guinea,
Australia, and surrounding
tropical islands. Close relatives of
swallowtails, birdwings fly to the
crowns of towering jungle trees and
are seldom encountered near the
ground. Female birdwings are
larger than males, some with
wingspans approaching eleven
inches. The sexes, moreover, are
differently colored. This male New
Guinea Birdwing (O. priamus
poseidon) *is typical, its velvety-*
black wings accented by broad
bands of intensely iridescent green.
The females lack such bright colors.
(Thomas W. Davies)

138 *overleaf. A Red-spotted Purple*
(Basilarchia astyanax) *suns on a*
zinnia in a Michigan garden. Like
the dark form of the female Tiger
Swallowtail, this butterfly protects
itself from predatory birds by
mimicking the colors of the noxious
Pipevine Swallowtail. The Red-
spotted Purple is found from New
England to the canyons of the
Southwest, in woodland, prairie,
and desert habitats. (Robert P.
Carr)

137

140. *No wildflower is more aptly named than butterfly weed, whose clusters of bright orange flowers attract hosts of butterflies and moths every summer. There will be more spectacular visitors to this showy milkweed, but no species will be as numerous as the little Coral Hairstreak (Harkenclenus titus), typically seen sitting with its wings folded as it sips nectar from the countless blossoms. Coral Hairstreaks occur throughout the United States and Canada, from open meadows in the East and Midwest to mountain canyons in the Far West.* (John Shaw)

141 *top left. The spherical eggs of a Northern Pearly Eye (Enodia anthedon) are attached to a sedge— the larval food plant—in a damp woodland glade in Michigan. The female Northern Pearly Eye, one of the small butterflies known as satyrs or wood nymphs, lays its eggs in pairs that are dispersed over a large area to avoid discovery by parasitic ichneumon wasps.* (Larry West)

141 *top right. Sumacs are one favored nectar source for the Red-banded Hairstreak (Calycopis cecrops), an abundant species along the Gulf Coast. These small butterflies, with a wingspan of just one inch, are especially active at dusk. Hairstreaks belong to the family Lycaenidae, the gossamer wings, with some 7,000 species worldwide.* (Larry West)

141 *bottom. Most North American hairstreaks are rather plain little butterflies—brownish with perhaps a few eye-catching flashes of color. But in the New World tropics one can find hairstreaks as brightly painted as more famous species. The Regal Hairstreak (Evenus regalis), occurring from Mexico to northern South America, certainly earns its name. Hairstreaks are so named for the fine lines on the underside of their wings.* (Harry N. Darrow)

142 *overleaf. The Zebra Longwing (Heliconius charitonius) is the most famous resident insect among the celebrated wildlife species found in Florida's Everglades National Park. At dusk, these distinctively marked butterflies assemble at communal roosts in hammocks and thickets in the vast sea of grass. Zebra Longwings are found from the southern United States to Latin America and the West Indies. Like other butterflies in the family Heliconiidae, their caterpillars feed on the toxic leaves of passion flowers, making them noxious to predators and subject to mimicry by other butterflies.* (Harry N. Darrow)

144. *The larva of a leaf-mining moth,* Phyllocnistis populiella, *feeds on an aspen leaf in the mountains of Wyoming. The tiny caterpillar is clearly visible at the head of its mine. The leaf surface appears silvery where tissue has been eaten away, while the dark center line is a trail of feces left by the caterpillar since it emerged from the egg. Leaf-mining larvae are remarkably adapted for life inside a leaf: the head and body are flattened, the legs are vestigial or absent altogether, and they are equipped with protruding jaws that slice away the soft internal tissue. Some species even pupate inside the leaf. Leaf-mining moths can be identified both by the distinctive shape of the mine and by the host plant, since each species attacks a single kind or group of closely related plants.* (C. Allan Morgan)

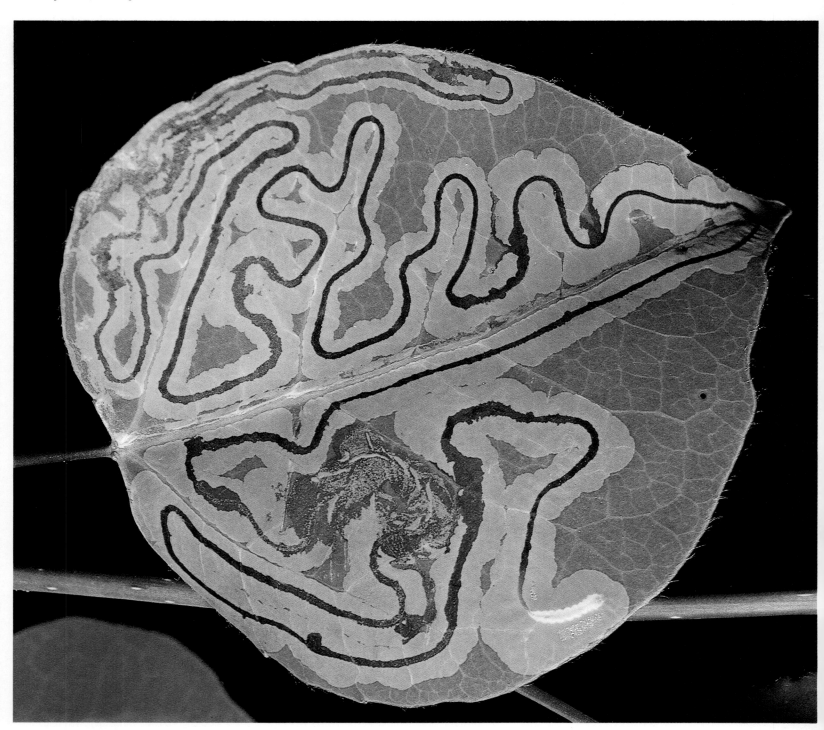

The Luna
And Other Moths

Around and around it circled, as though tied to the streetlamp by an invisible tether. Would it ever tire of this endless circling? Suddenly the big moth changed its course and settled on the wooden pole a few feet lower than the lamp. For a moment it raised and lowered its pale green wings, then drooped them, overlapping them gracefully and pressing them against the wood. Then the long narrow tails that curved from the border of the hind wings could be seen more distinctly than before, when they had been fluttering ribbons behind the flying moth. Those tails and the pastel-green color of the insect identified it as a Luna Moth (*Actias luna*)—a "moon moth"—perhaps the most famous among the giant silkworm moths (Saturniidae). Its 4½–inch wingspan, together with the delicate wing coloration and the added grace of its tails, make it as conspicuous a night flier as can be met with in the eastern half of North America. Only Asia has similar moths.

The moth on the lamp pole was a female with almost threadlike antennae and a swollen abdomen. She had emerged just hours before from a thin, brown pupal skin concealed by a cocoon of brown silk partly surrounded by a curled dead leaf and lying on the ground at the foot of a walnut tree. That was as far as the insect had traveled as a caterpillar, after descending from the top of the same tree. The tree's foliage provided all the nourishment the caterpillar needed to grow from hatching size to a length of 3⅛ inches. The sausage-shaped creature bore small spiny tubercles, a narrow yellow stripe along each side, and some long fine hair.

The Luna Moth could not know that her future was in doubt because of deforestation and the widespread use of pesticides. If she was aware of anything, it was that she should have a mate. Contracting a few muscles in her abdomen, she began to release her potent perfume. Almost undetectable by humans, the fragrance was wafted by the night air, creating a cone-shaped area of fragrance that reached halfway up the trees and down to the ground.

Half a mile away, a smaller Luna Moth was clinging to a tree, waving his feathery antennae to sample the night air. The perfume of the female reached him and he flew into it, zigging and zagging upwind, turning back into the fragrant zone every time he reached its edge. Progressively he approached the female Luna on the pole. He circled the distracting light several times before settling close to the source of that tantalizing aroma. She waved her wings at him, and he crawled over to rub against her. She moved away. He followed.

Soon the female Luna began to respond to a different inner urge. She must deposit her fertilized eggs in a suitable place, just a few on an appropriate tree. She would know the right trees by the odor—they would be hickory or birch, or, in southern states, sweet gum or persimmon. She would unwittingly choose trees on which few giant silkworm moths other than Lunas deposit their eggs. Her caterpillars would thus meet a minimum of competition for the proper food. Her actions would make them specialists, even though they could just as well digest the foliage of most other trees.

The suburban community in which the Luna Moths emerge also produces a dozen other giant silkworm moths of different kinds during the usual summer. Few people see them because they fly high into the treetops soon after emerging from their cocoons. Most of these moths are of one species; they come out of tough egg-shaped cocoons usually found lying on the ground below maple, sycamore, basswood, and chestnut; some are found below alders in a swampy region. As caterpillars, growing to 3½ inches long, they are bright green with yellow bands and red and silver tubercles. After pupating, they emerge as brownish-yellow Polyphemus Moths (*Antheraea polyphemus*), with a conspicuous eyespot on each hind wing and no tails.

The Polyphemus caterpillars never have to compete

with the larvae of a Cecropia Moth (*Hyalophora cecropia*) because the latter spend their early lives on ash, elm, willow, and lilac—the only places where the adult deposits its eggs. A Cecropia caterpillar is green too, with bluish shading along the sides and a great many red, yellow, and blue tubercles. When fully grown, it descends from its tree to spin its cocoon in some shrub, enclosing lengthwise a strong twig that will support the cocoon all winter while the pupa becomes a moth.

On spicebush, sassafras, and other shrubs, the bluish-green caterpillars of the Promethia Moth (*Callosamia promethia*) seem equally provident as they get ready to pupate. First they spin a strong mesh of silk around a stem where an appropriate leaf is attached, then more silk around and inside the curl of the leaf until it is tethered to the shrub and ready to be closed off as a private chamber for the winter. After the caterpillar pupates inside this hideaway, it may complete its transformation and be ready to emerge the following summer, or it may dawdle throughout an extra year or two. This delay often safeguards the species against a failure of food plants for the caterpillars in any one year. Over successive years, a generation of adults will emerge, mate, and distribute eggs. Nature uses this simple system to hedge her bets.

The giant silkworm moths come from the biggest cocoons, with the most silk, although no one has succeeded in making the material a commercial source of fiber. The emerging adults include the most spectacular night fliers all over the world. The Atlas Moth (*Attacus atlas*) of Asia, with a wingspan as great as ten inches, may have the greatest wing area of any insect. The Comet's Tail (*Argema mittrei*) of Madagascar has hind wings with brown tails almost four inches long—as great as the spread of its brown fore wings. Yet not every individual of a large species is of giant size. Some are only half as big because, as caterpillars, they did not find much to eat, or obvious danger kept them from feeding even at night; sometimes an upset in their hormones induced them to pupate before they had completed their larval feeding program.

A surprising array of giant silkworm moths wear impressive eyespots on their wings, and can frighten away a bird, lizard, or monkey merely by suddenly exposing these black-centered, pale-ringed circles.

The smaller Io Moth (*Automeris io*) of North America, with wings spanning less than three inches, can flash a similar warning to predators, but holds it in reserve, usually showing only its brown or yellowish fore wings. As a caterpillar, the Io is far more formidable, with branching, venomous spines along its back and sides.

As earthbound creatures, we meet the giant silkworm moths of the treetops only sporadically and accidentally. They are a fluttery lot and make no great effort to escape us, perhaps because their ancestors have met few humans. Far more alert and elusive are the underwing moths (chiefly *Catocala* spp.) that rest on the bark of trees or other neutral backgrounds within human reach. Each underwing moth conceals the bright pink, yellow, or white curved markings on its dark hind wings by spreading them flat against the support, then drawing together over them the broad fore wings whose fine markings in gray and black camouflage the creature against the bark. If the concealing pattern succeeds, a bird or person passes by without noticing the moth and it is safe. A moment's hesitation alarms the insect, and it spreads its fore wings, exposing the shocking colors underneath. Any closer approach and the underwing leaps into flight, to speed away on an erratic course between the tree trunks to another resting place. An aficionado of underwings has to be quick and competent to catch up with one of these beauties before it gets away.

We hardly expect underwings to be so alert and timid, for they are members of mothdom's largest family, the Noctuidae. The family includes many undistinguished "millers," always ready to shed pale scales like so much dusty flour if we disturb them where they cling. The only common name for the whole group is owlets, although only a few of them have eyespots or anything else that might suggest an owl. Their caterpillars include cutworms, which fell seedling plants by biting the young stem and eating a little of the freshly exposed tissue. Other larvae in the group bore into stems and roots, or feed on decayed organic matter; still others, surprisingly enough, are cannibalistic.

Many of the owlets have one ability that makes them outstanding. They have fine hearing organs on each side of the body, close to the wing bases, which they use to detect ultrasonic messages. The organs are bat detectors, alerting the moth to the approach of an echo-locating bat. Down plunges the moth, to hide silently on some support, while the bat flies on until it is heard no more. The performance reminds one of a motorist whose small black box enables him to escape a radar trap.

The greatest wingspan of any modern insect belongs to an owlet of tropical America, the Agrippina Moth (*Thysania agrippina*), which is seldom less than nine inches across and often more than twelve. How elated we were to discover one of these giants in the rainforest of Panama, where the insect's wings were spread flat against the smooth trunk of a huge tree. Carefully we fitted together the parts of a collapsible butterfly net and reached up on tiptoe to strike the net ring over the wonderful moth. We fully expected it to flutter into the soft mesh bag and let us examine it at close range. Instead, the Agrippina slithered between the curve of the tree trunk and the steel ring of the net, then rushed to some safer site deep in the jungle. We could agree with other explorers that the flight of Agrippina is batlike and swift, yet we noticed no contrast between the upper surface of the moth's great gray wings and the underside. Not until much later, in a museum, did we discover that the underside—which the insect pressed against the tree —is bright steel-blue, right out to the scalloped margins. Perhaps this color is required for another life-saving trick that the huge moth can perform when its normal habits fail to provide it with safety or enough concealment.

We are always surprised to see moths active in daylight hours. Their threadlike antennae, neither clubbed nor hooked near the tip, prove that they are not butterflies no matter how bright their colors. The Rattlebox Moth (*Utetheisa bella*) of the American Southeast and Texas is a master of disappearance. By day the moth flits along, displaying bright pink hind wings with an irregular black outer border, and orange to yellow fore wings, speckled with black on small areas of white. The moth settles on a weed and wraps its wings around the support. No pink shows, and the speckled fore wings blend perfectly in the moth's surroundings. The caterpillar, which feeds on rattlebox, sweet clover, or sweet fern, is far more conspicuous with its red head, yellow body, white side stripes, and alternating black and white along the back.

The Lichen Moth (*Lycomorpha pholus*) of North America seems doubly unusual. Its caterpillar feeds on lichens, which most insects shun, and resembles a lichen in its color and rough surface. The adult Lichen Moth is very similar in color, pattern, size, and actions to some of the netwing beetles, with which it associates on flowers; in fact, one can easily be mistaken for the other.

Both of these day-flying moths are tiger moths (Arctiidae), close kin to many nocturnal kinds that commonly fly to artificial lights. It was one of the night-active tiger moths that Keats had in mind when he wrote,

All diamonded with panes of quaint device,
Innumerable of stains, and splendid dyes,
As are the Tiger Moth's deep damask wings.

Best known of the tiger moths, although more familiar as a caterpillar than as an adult, is the brown and black Woolly Bear Moth (*Isia isabella*), the adult of the Woolly Bear caterpillar that is everyone's favorite. Followers of folklore insist that this insect forecasts the severity of the winter ahead according to the number of body segments concealed by bristly black hairs rather than rust-red ones. Actually, it is cold weather in early autumn that induces an immature Woolly Bear to start seeking winter shelter—at this time, the black zones fore and aft are more extensive than they will be when the caterpillar is fully grown. Many a Woolly Bear is still hungry when spring weather renews its alertness. The larva feeds on some roadside weeds before spinning its cocoon, stiffening it with bristles from its coat, and starting its pupal transformation.

We might paraphrase the old couplet to read, "What's a tiger moth? At best, it's just a caterpillar dressed." Somehow, when we get to know the larva and, later, the adult insect, they appear as quite different individuals. But then, we ourselves experience no transformation as complete as that survived by any moth. Almost certainly the insect has no memory of it either.

A special mystery surrounds some spectacular moths that act as bogus butterflies in the tropics from Indo-Australia to Central America. The hind wings of these striking beauties, members of the family Uraniidae, are edged conspicuously with white, and project into multiple "tails." The front wings dazzle the eye with alternating bands of metallic green and lustrous black. The most magnificent among them may be *Urania croesus* of Madagascar, which wears a flare of orange-red across both hind wings. *Urania riphius* of the American tropics, with a three- to four-inch wingspan, becomes particularly incredible when thousands of them fly rapidly side by side out to the open sea, with no land ahead as a stopping place. How can inherited behavior commit so many to a watery grave year after year?

Allen M. Young tried to count one of these aerial emigrations in Costa Rica, and reached a total of 54,625 individuals between sunrise and sundown on five consecutive days. Both sexes were represented, the females apparently all unmated and four-fifths of them bulging with eggs. Gentle breezes do not deflect their course, which often aims across thousands of miles of open ocean. How can a moth that flies like a butterfly make such a fatal mistake? Despite our awareness of this seemingly incomprehensible waste of life on one-way trips to nowhere, and despite the extraordinary abundance of the emigrants, the caterpillar stage of this handsome insect remains a mystery. Countless millions of them must eat the foliage of some vegetation high in the rainforest, among the dense canopy of interlacing limbs and vines beyond the reach of humankind. Many of the *Urania* moths must stay behind to sustain the population. Yet their whereabouts still remain unknown to entomologists.

It seems far less of a surprise that some of the wonderful sphinx moths (Sphingidae) should be active by day instead of by night. Some, with a wingspan of two inches or less, simply shed most of the scales that conceal the transparent membrane of their wings and, soon after escape from their pupal sites underground, visit flowers in sunlight as though they were bumblebees or hummingbirds. The Hummingbird Clearwing (*Hemaris thysbe*) is one such mimic, looking more like a hummingbird than a moth as it softly buzzes its outstretched wings while it sips nectar from bergamot or phlox.

Most sphinx moths spend the hours of daylight as motionless and inconspicuous as possible, and then hover by night on strong pointed wings before some pale flower, probing its depths for nectar with a tongue that is unusually long.

Tiny moths vastly exceed the giants in both variety

and number. A diverse assortment attain their full growth as caterpillars between the upper and lower surface of a single leaf. The caterpillar eats out a narrow irregular strip of green tissue, thus earning the epithet "miner." Some kinds both pupate and overwinter inside the leaf. Others escape, let themselves down to ground level on a silken thread spun from saliva, and pupate underground during the winter. Each of these tiny insects emerges as a truly miniature moth, a "micro" with a body less than a tenth of an inch long and a wingspan of barely a quarter-inch. These "micros" may be smaller than the old-fashioned Clothes Moths (*Tineola bisselliella* or *Tinea pellionella*), yet every scale will contribute to a distinctive pattern, a fragile beauty that is often seen best with a magnifying lens.

Some of the caterpillars that let themselves down from a tree to the ground on a supporting strand of silk are members of macro, not micro, families. Many are loopers or measuring worms (Geometridae), which travel on flat surfaces by alternately straightening and arching their backs to bring the two or four soft, stumpy, leglike organs (prolegs) on the hindmost segments up close to the six true legs at the front end. Loopers lack intermediate prolegs on which to move more gradually, and this makes them easily recognizable. They feed on many different plants and transform into moths with broad and flimsy wings that span from ⅜ to 2½ inches. Most of them have a bat detector on each side of the abdomen and a habit of resting with their wings spread out to each side, making all four clearly visible. Many of their caterpillars can disappear simply by clinging to a branch with the hindmost prolegs, while raising the rest of the body stiffly in a pose suggesting a leafless twig. The caterpillar may not be able to eat all day while exploiting this fortuitous resemblance, but maintaining its motionless posture improves its chances of surviving until nightfall.

153. *The larva of a lappet moth,* Tolype velleda, *makes its way along the rain-slicked trunk of a sycamore tree in Michigan. These caterpillars, named for the small lobes or "lappets" on the sides of each body segment, are commonly found on apple and poplar trees and lilac bushes. Another species,* Tolype laricis, *frequents larches and pines. Lappet moths belong to the family Lasiocampidae, which includes the notorious American Tent Caterpillar Moth* (Malacosoma americanum), *whose larvae spin silken communal tents on the branches of apples, pears, and wild cherries, venturing forth to defoliate and sometimes kill the host trees.* (Robert P. Carr)

154. *A newly hatched caterpillar of the Privet Sphinx Moth* (Sphinx ligustri) *consumes its eggshell; a second larva nibbles the edge of the leaf, which holds two unhatched eggs. With a wingspan of four inches, the Privet Sphinx Moth is a well-known European representative of the Sphingidae, a cosmopolitan family of large and easily recognized moths. Day-flying sphinx moths often are mistaken for hummingbirds as they hover on blurred wings in front of flowers, sipping nectar with their long tongues. The Privet Sphinx Moth larva feeds largely on lilac and privet, an evergreen hedge shrub.* (Heather Angel/Biofotos)

155 *top right and bottom. A newly hatched Evergreen Bagworm* (Thyridopteryx ephemeraeformis) *builds a portable cocoon of silken threads and plant fibers, leaving only its head and thorax exposed. The caterpillar moves about on its thoracic legs only, enlarging the case—which is covered with bits of leaves and grass—as it grows. Feces are passed out an opening at the small end. Evergreen Bagworms are commonly found on cedars in warmer parts of North America, but they defoliate sycamores and other deciduous trees as well. The bag may be 2½ inches long by the time the caterpillar fastens the cocoon to a branch and pupates. Only the males are transformed into winged moths; the larvalike females remain in their bags, where they mate through the opening, lay their eggs, and die.* (Top right Betty Randall; *bottom* Robert W. Mitchell)

155 *top left. The caterpillar of the Banana Leaf-rolling Moth* (Erionota thrax) *from Malaysia chews a cut parallel to the rib of a banana leaf. The nearly severed section hangs down in a coil that the larva occupies for protection against predators, parasites, and weather extremes.* (Ivan Polunin)

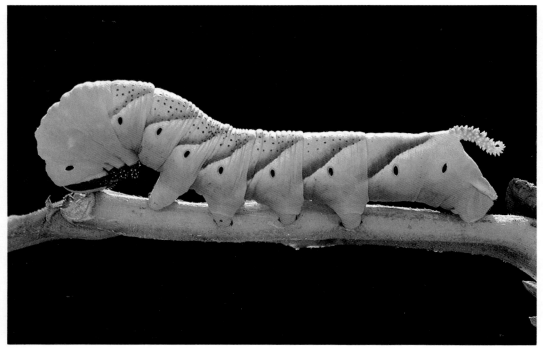

156 *top. Like many sphinx moth larvae, the Willow Hornworm (Smerinthus cerisyi) has a prominent, backward-pointing horn on the rear end of its abdomen. But the horn is merely ornamental and of no use as a weapon. The diagonal yellow lines on the caterpillar's body effectively mimic the veins of a leaf. As its name suggests, this species is found on river bottom willows across the northern United States and Canada.* (Edward S. Ross)

156 *center. The Death's-head Sphinx Moth (Acherontia atropos) of Africa and Europe is named for a skull-like design on the thorax of the adult. Appropriately, the generic name derives from Acheron —a mythical river in Hades—and according to superstition, the moth's appearance presages death. To complete the image, the larvae feed on poisonous belladonna and nightshade. The Death's-head has a short, strong, and pointed tongue with which it pierces the combs of bees to suck out honey. To avoid being stung on its nocturnal visits to beehives, the moth emits a beelike chirping noise that inhibits the aggressiveness of the workers.* (Michel Viard/Jacana)

156 *bottom. The caterpillar of a Cecropia Moth* (Hyalophora cecropia) *munches on a maple leaf. Simply stated, the larvae of moths and butterflies are eating machines. Their powerful mandibles make quick work of greenery, and even wood. Nearly blind, they have mouthparts that are sensitive to touch and taste, guiding them to the right food sources. With a wingspan of nearly six inches, the Cecropia is North America's largest moth. Its five-inch caterpillars are found on a wide variety of trees and shrubs.* (Lynn M. Stone)

157. *Faced by a predator, the caterpillar of a fruit-sucking moth,* Orthreis fullonia, *will thrash from side to side, amplifying the threat implied by its goblinlike eyespots. Found in Australia and across tropical Africa and Asia, this moth can pierce the rinds of citrus fruit, mangoes, and melons to suck out the juices.* (Stanley Breeden)

158 *overleaf. A Hummingbird Clearwing* (Hemaris thysbe) *drinks nectar from milkweed flowers in a New York meadow. The large bodies of these sphinx moths are packed with muscles that power the long, narrow front wings. When they are formed in the pupa, the wings of this day-flying moth are fully covered with scales; but the scales are shed soon after the moth emerges, leaving its wings largely transparent.* (Adrian J. Dignan)

160. *A sphinx moth,* Deilephila hypothous, *in the New Guinea jungle, presents a fine example of what entomologists call "coincident disruptive markings." Pale lines on the moth's wings cross its thorax, aiding camouflage. Eyespots on the wings, meanwhile, are designed to spook predators. Moths of the family Sphingidae are vital pollinators of many flowering plants, including orchids. They are so named because the caterpillar rests with its head and forepart reared up in a position that suggests the Egyptian Sphinx.* (Thomas W. Davies)

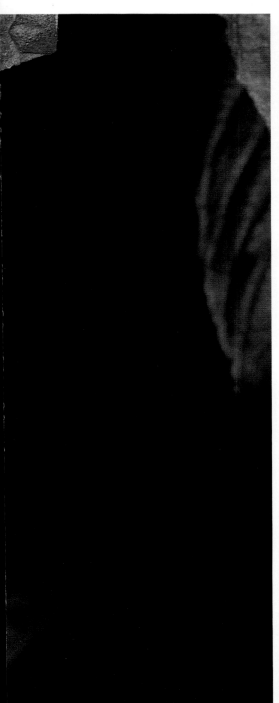

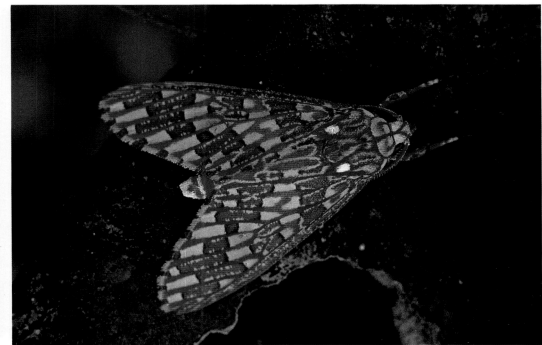

161 *top and bottom. The bright colors and bold patterns of these tiger moths—*Evius albiscripta, *top;* Idalus rubens, *bottom—in the Amazon rainforest undoubtedly advertise repugnant taste to would-be predators. Tiger moths of the family Arctiidae occur throughout the world, and many contain toxic substances that quickly educate their enemies. Tiger moth caterpillars are often hairy; famous among them is the Woolly Bear (*Isia isabella*) found across North America. According to legend, wide black bands on its bristly coat foretell a severe winter. (Both* Kjell B. Sandved)*

162 *overleaf. One of the giant silkworm moths of the family Saturniidae, the Cynthia Moth (*Samia cynthia*) was brought to Philadelphia from China in 1861 in the mistaken hope that its thick cocoons would be as valuable commercially as those of the true silkworm,* Bombyx mori. *The Cynthia's food plant was also introduced into North America— the ailanthus, or tree-of-heaven, a hardy weed tree that now thrives in vacant lots, backyards, and waste places in much of temperate North America. (Rod Planck)*

164. *The Blue-green Darner* (Aeschna cyanea) *belongs to a family of large, high- and fast-flying dragonflies aptly called "mosquito hawks," for they zip in and out of swarms of midges and mosquitoes, capturing prey in a basket formed by their spine-covered legs and eating on the wing. Darners are typically blue, green, or brown, with clear wings that span up to six inches. Scouring the skies over the ponds and swamps from which they emerged, darners hunt down flying insects of all sizes, even other dragonflies. Their own enemies are insect-eating birds, including small falcons.* (Klaus Paysan)

Water Sprites

One can sit on the shore of a pond or a slowly winding
stream, relaxing while the city's impatient tempo
drains away; thoughts come out and sun themselves.
As Thoreau came to realize beside Walden Pond, "It
is a soothing employment, on one of those fine days
in the fall when all the warmth of the sun is fully
appreciated, to sit on a stump . . . overlooking
the pond, and study the dimpling circles which are
incessantly inscribed on its otherwise invisible
surface . . . Not a fish can leap or an insect fall on the
pond but it is thus reported . . . in lines of beauty."
Thoreau did not mention the experience that anyone
can have in such a place, when adult water sprites
come and settle on a leg, an arm, or a bush close at
hand. If we sit quietly, they do not take fright, or
even notice that we are alive.
The first visitor may be a slender damselfly, one of
dozens that flit along the water margin. It settles on
all six of its short, slender legs, holding its abdomen
stiffly horizontal or parallel to its support, wrapped
gently by four narrow wings. They fold together
inconspicuously. The damsel's head seems mostly to
consist of two knobby eyes which project to the sides
and give the creature vision in almost all directions.
Male damselflies watch alertly for others of their kind
and color pattern. Any newcomer is a potential mate,
but only a close look and perhaps a whiff of perfume
will tell him for sure that a female is suitable. If he
can win her cooperation, she will permit him to grasp
her slender neck in a pair of pincerlike appendages at
his tail tip. Off the two fly in tandem. After her eggs
have been fertilized and are ready for laying, the pair

alights at the water's edge. The female backs down into the water. The male holds on and remains mostly above the surface. When her eggs have been deposited, the female will start upward while the male pulls. He flutters his wings until the efforts of the two of them bring the female out of the water to dry off and fly away.

Some females insist on going deeper before they start laying. When the male has been pulled down as far as he will go, he releases his mate. He either hovers over the spot until she reappears or settles on some twig nearby to keep watch. This is dangerous for the female since, if she takes too long, her mate may abandon her to court another damselfly, leaving his first mate to drown.

Damselflies and dragonflies uniformly spend all their immature lives below the surface of fresh water. Only the more delicate—the damsels—reenter a body of water after reaching maturity. Dragonflies wet only the tip of the abdomen, either while standing on some secure support or while flying above a pond or stream. Their antics while they attend to these procreative enterprises add much movement, color, and brilliance to the scene viewed from shore. Males of the larger dragonflies, with wingspans of four inches or more, often patrol particular lengths of shoreline as territories from which any other male of their species is to be chased out as an intruder. A female is welcomed until the courting dragonfly, perhaps detecting some encouragement from his potential mate, reaches his abdominal tip far forward below his body and places a small packet of sperm cells in a pocket close to his hindmost pair of legs. Thereafter he grasps his mate with claspers at his abdominal tip, closed around her short, slender neck. He flies ahead; she follows, unable to get free until she has done her part. In flight she must reach forward with her own abdominal tip, pick out the packet of sperm from his special pocket, and use them to fertilize her eggs. For a while the two wing their way along as a "mating wheel" like no other in the animal kingdom. Then, still flying behind him, she droops the tip of her abdomen. The two descend without slowing until she can wash off the eggs extruded in sequence. The combined momentum of the insects overcomes the drag of the water's surface film.

Once immersed, the egg of a damselfly or a dragonfly

can hatch on its own, releasing a strange little naiad with an enormous, underhanging lower lip. The naiad creeps about slowly in search of mosquito wrigglers and other prey. Detecting something suitable within range, the naiad reaches forward suddenly with its underlip and pulls the captive into its jaws. A damsel naiad must clamber with all six legs to approach a meal, trailing its leaflike gill plates behind, while a dragonfly naiad can jet-propel itself by expelling water from a capacious chamber in its posterior end where its gills are secluded. The breadth of the abdomen of the dragonfly naiad creates the space for this water-filled chamber.

Continuous hunger seems a unifying feature of damselflies and dragonflies, both immature and adult. Satisfying this urge keeps the naiads active, busily devouring meals of many kinds, composed of almost anything they can subdue: other insects, mites, crustaceans, hatchling fishes, tadpoles, and worms. Hunger may keep an adult damselfly hovering with surprising skill just far enough from a slanting plant stem to be able to pick off, chew, and swallow individual aphids one after another. We can watch this performance at close range without disturbing the damsel, but it is rarely so easy to see a feeding dragonfly at work. After a fast and twisting pursuit, the dragon catches its prey, holding it tightly among its legs. Just occasionally, when a dragonfly settles at close range, it is still holding its latest victim as though its legs were a shopping basket. The dragon's head swivels and nods while its jaws pick out the edible parts of the captive. Rarely does the meal last a minute. Then the dragon is ready for more. The dedicated "dragonfly man," Professor James G. Needham of Cornell University, decided to learn how many flies a large dragonfly would eat in one meal. He provided a captive dragon with one house fly after another, as fast as it could consume them; but he ran out of flies, and patience, while the dragon was still eager. Its digestive tract processed the flies as fast as the dragonfly could swallow. Apparently, the insect was insatiable, even though it lacked exercise or the possibility of growing larger. Since the ever-hungry dragon was a male, Professor Needham could not even credit the insect with storing some of its overabundant nourishment in eggs for the welfare of a coming generation.

Like dragonfly and damselfly naiads, the flat-bodied

naiads of stoneflies and the caterpillarlike larvae (caddisworms) of caddisflies are committed to aquatic life when immature. Stoneflies and some caddisflies hatch from eggs inserted underwater by females that routinely dip their tail tips or dunk themselves to penetrate the surface film. Other females, of the caddisfly family Phryganeidae, are exceptional in producing a doughnut-shaped ring of eggs embedded in jelly, which they manage to shape around the end of a branch of some tree or shrub overhanging the water. Hatchlings tumble from their egg ring and plummet straight through the surface film, fully ready to survive in water.

Stonefly naiads cling tightly to stones in a riffle, pressing as close as possible to this support while prowling for food. Weaker insects and other sorts of prey sustain the naiad until its wings, which have developed within flat pads atop its back, are ready to break free and expand for use in the air. Turbulence in the water helps many a stonefly naiad to escape into air, there to shed its skin a final time, explosively becoming an adult.

Some stoneflies emerge to disperse and reproduce in almost any month of the year, as though underwater they had lost track of night length and every other ordinary cue to season and calendar. Slender, black, half-inch naiads of *Capnia vernalis* creep out onto snowbanks in midwinter. During the summer, much larger ones become lost by flying to artificial lights. A majority go no farther in their feeble flight than to a resting site atop or below a green leaf overhanging the stream in which they spent their weeks of immaturity. We notice them there by the dozen, waiting for dusk and the hour to start a swarming dance above some tree or shrub. Each female flies into the swarm of dancing males and is caught by one. The pair settles on a leaf to mate; eventually, when she has eggs to be rinsed off, the female returns to the water's edge.

Mayflies (Ephemeroptera) are equally adept at finding food as naiads under water, getting their wing pads ready for a sudden transformation, then bursting into air and flight as though long experience had taught them how to accomplish the change most dexterously. Naiads of the largest mayflies make shallow burrows in the muddy bottom of lakes and require more than a year to reach full size. Tusklike mouthparts help them force their way through the ooze in search of edible organic matter. Somehow all of the individuals nearing two years of age attain the same critical growth stage almost simultaneously. All of them cease feeding and, within a few days of one another, swim upward at night to escape into the air. Flashing forth their smoky wings, they fly to some dry support—if they can find it. For a few hours they will settle there, fasting while completing their preparations for maturity. Unlike any other insect, they will shed their skins once more after expanding their wings. Out will come a true adult with shiny, transparent wings—a large triangular fore pair and a tiny hind pair—and fragile tails much longer than the antennae.

Once their flying organs are dry, the males can begin their mating dance in the air. Up and back and down and forward they go in endless loops until some female flies into the swarm and comes within snatching distance. The aerial ballet may last all night and can exhaust the food reserves stored by the naiad before emerging. The adults eat nothing, and die when their dance is done.

The winged existence of mayflies of all kinds, including those that browse on films of algae coating rocks in riffles and underwater vegetation in slower streams, lasts only hours or, at most, a day. The ancient Greeks became aware of this phenomenon and described it by the word *ephemeros*—lasting only a day. The mayflies were given the order name Ephemeroptera because of their exceptionally brief winged existence.

The ancestry of mayflies, damselflies, and dragonflies can be traced, with few changes in body form, back to the beginning of the insect fossil record. A few preserved remains of their naiad stages have just been uncovered in Europe. Stoneflies appear a little later among the treasures of the paleo-entomologist, and caddisflies much more recently, as befits the occurrence of a pupal transformation during their development. Insects of no other order are so uniformly aquatic while young, although individual species and genera have found a way to benefit from underwater life.

Most caddisworms construct a movable shelter from plant fragments, a kind of tubular hideaway. Body movements of the caddisworm pump water in and through the case, which rests on the bottom or is tied with silken salivary strands to some firm object such as a stone. Caddisworms of the genus *Triaenodes* construct such lightweight spiral tubes of plant material that they can swim slowly from place to place, vigorously waving their front legs while holding on to the case with special hooks on the soft prolegs at the posterior end. Larvae of the genus *Brachycentrus* build tapering shelters, square in cross section, and anchor them to stones in riffles; then they position themselves at the upstream doorway with legs widespread to capture any edible morsel the current brings.

Active caddisworms of the genus *Rhyacophila* build no case at all until one is required as a shelter for the pupal transformation; these insects prowl along streambottoms and over stones in riffles, looking for prey and overcoming it without being washed downstream. Caddisworms of the genus *Hydropsyche* are also uncased, but weave bag-shaped nets of salivary silk and attach them to rocks, where the current will bring them a succession of meals. Caddisworms of many families produce movable cases of different materials—sand, pebbles, tiny snail shells, or even opals and garnets in some streams of the American Southwest. The Log Cabin Builder (*Limnephilus rhombicus*) inhabits temporary pools in forest regions of the eastern United States and adjacent Canada. There it cuts slender twigs and fallen pine needles into lengths of less than a half-inch and fastens them together crosswise to create a shaggy shelter. In each instance, the case becomes a cocoon after the caddisworm has eaten its fill and is ready to transform. Following a larval life spent nourishing itself on minute algae scraped from underwater objects, the caddis can fast during its pupal transformation and all through its exciting escape from the case and from the water. As an adult it will eat nothing while flying about, resting, finding a mate and propagating its species.

Many a caddisworm is devoured, case and all, by fish. The indigestible case materials may be unwanted ballast. Fish also try to catch emerging caddisflies or females that come to the water to lay eggs. Anglers find that an artificial fly, tied with imagination and skill to resemble an adult caddisfly on the wing, will entice a trout to swallow a hook and end the food chain as a fisherman's dinner.

A very small number—just a few species, in fact— actually invade the saline world of the sea. One New

Zealand caddisworm, a species of *Philanisus*, makes its cases out of fragments of seaweed. One water strider of the genus *Halobates* ventures far from quiet lagoon waters among mangrove roots to ride the open ocean. The sea-going strider lays its eggs on rafts no more substantial than the floating feathers dropped by seabirds. A few insects, mostly fly larvae, tolerate the hot water in thermal springs and eat heat-resistant algae there. Surely, it took eons for the ancestors of these water sprites to learn survival in such unlikely situations.

The speed with which dragonflies, damselflies, stoneflies, and mayflies transform from the aquatic, immature stage to the aerial adult gives a patient scientist a good chance to recognize one individual before and after the transformation. Where the change requires weeks or months, as it does in members of many orders, identifying the young to species is generally difficult since the scientific names are regularly given to adults. After a dragonfly, a damselfly, or a stonefly has emerged from its naiad skin, the skin itself retains much of its former form and all of its structural details, and can be a valuable reference tool.

Indeed, the empty skin remains quite often in a natural setting as evidence that its former inhabitant has escaped and might be nearby. Dozens of dragonfly naiads may climb the weathered side of a wooden boathouse and cling beneath its eaves while shedding their skins and emerging as adults. Months or years later, the empty skins may still be found where they were abandoned—often an expert can identify them even then. Similar empty skins left by stoneflies on a rock wall above a fast stream tell a specialist exactly what kinds of adults live in the region, even if the season is not right for a single stonefly to be found alive.

Many of the caddisworms leave behind still more information as they begin their transformation to adulthood. Each caddisworm uses the last of its salivary silk to spin a grating or grillwork at each end of its case. Water can still flow through, bringing dissolved oxygen and carrying away carbon dioxide in solution. Then the caddisworm sheds its larval skin —hard plates, head capsule, bristles, and all—and stuffs these wastes in a corner, out of the way. A knowledgeable scientist can identify the pupa because the pupal covering reveals on the outside how many movable spurs the adult will carry on each leg, the form of the mouthparts and feet, the length of the antennae, and other distinctive features. From an examination of the maturing pupa as well as the discarded larval skin, the entomologist can associate the adult and immature of the species with complete confidence. A single specimen has provided all the information, and enclosed it in a neat container as reliably as though it were a document sent by registered mail.

Not all caddisworms are quite so provident. The net-weaving *Hydropsyche* caddisworm prepares only a loose shelter between stones for the first part of its pupal transformation. It retains the option of escaping a few minutes before being ready to emerge as an adult. The pupa suddenly becomes active, freeing the adult legs as swimming organs, then propelling itself up through fast water to the surface film and popping into the air at the same instant that the wings suddenly unfold and expand to full size. Away flits the caddisfly to find a secluded resting place, where its adult body can dry off and its body covering firm up to final form.

Bats by night, swallows by day, and other insect-eaters seem always ready to decimate the numbers of water sprites as they make this sudden step from early life in the water to maturity in the air. If the stream is flowing quickly, perhaps tumbling over a waterfall, the insect may be so busy coping with its change in environment that being wary of flying predators is just an extra burden. At the moment of its greatest vigor and while loaded with nourishment for its final contribution to posterity, the water sprite may be snapped up, benefitting only some quite different form of life. Perhaps the mayflies show the way this challenge can best be met: they emerge in such fantastic numbers that all the local insect-eaters go home satiated, unable to swallow another one. The rest of the mayflies are free to go where opportunity leads them, and keep this ancient way of life in continued operation.

173. *Two copulating pairs of narrow-winged damselflies,* Ischnura elegans, *cling to a reed. Dragonflies and damselflies mate both on the wing and at rest, forming a wheel in which the male locks claspers at the tip of his abdomen on the neck of the female. His mate, in turn, uses the tip of her abdomen to pick up a sperm packet from a chamber in the male's second abdominal segment. The female damselfly deposits her eggs in the tissue of submerged vegetation, sometimes diving beneath the surface. The female dragonfly typically skims the pond to brush off her eggs, which sink to the bottom.* (Michel Casino/Jacana)

174 *overleaf. A squadron of narrow-winged damselflies,* Coenagrion lindeni, *decorate a clear pond with their bright-blue bodies. At rest, most damselflies hold their wings together above the body; dragonflies, in contrast, hold their wings outstretched horizontally. Both have loosely attached heads that rotate freely, enabling the insects to see in all directions with their enormous eyes.* (Cyril de Klemm/Jacana)

176. *A Green Darner* (Anax junius) *emerges from its nymphal skin. It is midnight in a Michigan marsh; no insect-eating songbird is awake, and the larva has crawled three feet up a cattail stem to be safe from hungry frogs. By dawn the darner's wings will be dry and hard and it can join the aerial chase. Generations of children have been afraid of dragonflies because of an old folk tale that these "darning needles" would sew up the ears and lips of errant boys and girls.* (Larry West)

177 *top and bottom. Dragonflies and damselflies are rightfully famous for their beauty and their brilliant colors. None is more spectacular than the Red Skimmer* (Libellula saturata), *with its richly veined, four-inch wingspan. A familiar sight around stagnant ponds in Texas, Red Skimmers are territorial, the male defending an area while a female he has mated with deposits her eggs. A male may defend a territory for several weeks, mating with a succession of females.* (*Both* Robert W. Mitchell)

178 *overleaf. Sparkling beads of dew cover the wings and body of a red meadow dragonfly* (Sympetrum sp.) *in a Michigan prairie. Skimmers of this genus are among the smallest of North American dragonflies; some have wingspans of less than two inches. Red meadow dragonflies are abundant in late summer and autumn, congregating in large numbers at sunny spots near ponds and slow-moving streams.* (Larry West)

180. *A green lacewing,* Chrysopa carnea, *gleans aphids from a lettuce leaf. Common but lovely, lacewings are also known as "goldeneyes" for their large lustrous eyes, and "stinkflies" because they emit a putrid odor if touched—in defense against their enemies. At twilight in summer, masses of green lacewings swarm about streetlights and store windows.* Chrysopa carnea, *a familiar species in Europe and North America, invades houses at the onset of cold weather. A lowered rate of metabolism causes its color to change from green to red until the insect becomes active again in spring.* (Heather Angel/Biofotos)

On Wings of Lace

Early in the evening when the air is calm, and again after dawn before a breeze develops, the net-veined insects venture forth into gardens and fields. Their fluttery wings and feeble flight can cope with no wind, yet they have colonized every continent. Most enchanting of these creatures are the green lacewings (Chrysopidae). The pastel-green, paddle-shaped wings beat ineffectively, folding rooflike and transparent over the insect's back when it settles on some support. Bulging eyes of bright gold or copper add a striking detail that makes a green lacewing an attractive model for any artist. All green lacewings are much the same size, with a wingspan of about an inch. When we find a lacewing languishing in the house, usually on a window frame, we pick it up as gently as possible and release it outside. It is our favorite representative of the insect order Neuroptera (literally, the net-wings)—the order most uniformly beneficial to humans.

So voracious are the young of green lacewings as they prey upon aphids, mealybugs, and other agricultural pests that they are known as aphid-lions. Horticulturists in California raise thousands of one kind, *Chrysopa californica*, found west of the Rocky Mountains, and release them in greenhouses. An adult female green lacewing discourages cannibalism among her own young by stretching a thin silken stalk between a support and each egg she lays. Every hatchling tumbles past its siblings and starts hunting elsewhere on its own. Its squat, compact body glides about on short legs, like a forklift truck with sickle-shaped jaws projecting ahead. After destroying hundreds of small soft-bodied insects, the larva spins an egg-shaped silken cocoon on some leaf, whence it will later emerge as the delicate creature we admire.

Brown lacewings (Hemerobiidae) are mostly smaller, often with spots on their gauzy wings. They fly more frequently than green lacewings to artificial lights. Elsewhere they appear and disappear without much notice. Evelyn Cheesman described one that she saw blown by a steady gale, seemingly from nowhere, onto the ship she was riding at least sixty miles from the nearest land, in Geelvink Bay north of New Guinea. She disengaged the insect's foot that clung to a copra sack and moved the creature to a can. After one hour and forty minutes, "it was standing. If it had been a human being, we should consider it had been suffering from shock and had recovered."

Brown lacewings lay their eggs directly on a support, as though the hatchling larvae could be trusted not to eat all the unhatched eggs. Each larva vanishes soon after it has had a few meals, by attaching to hooked hairs on its own back the empty bodies of the prey it has devoured. It becomes a creeping morgue, perhaps unattractive to insect-eating birds but no less beneficial to human interests.

In Hawaii we meet the utmost paradox: a wingless lacewing. The flightless adults stay on the islands and reproduce, crawling from place to place without ever having to face a wind. By contrast, the warmer parts of the Old World contain spoon-winged lacewings (Nemopteridae), with gauzy hind wings improbably extended like ribbons with a flaring tip. A missionary brought us one he had picked up on a windowsill in Nigeria, but after his return to Africa he could not locate the unbelievable larval stage we had described to him. The larva builds a sand trap in the shape of a conical pit, then backs away from the bottom center until only its flat head and jaws await the arrival of some ant that blunders over the rim and down the slope. The larva has a slender neck three times as long as its head and jaws together, twice as long as its body, and much longer than its six slender legs. The creature keeps all of its legs buried in the sand as an anchor, in case the struggle to subdue a victim becomes intense.

Pit traps to catch edible animals have been used by men in Africa for thousands and thousands of years;

some are dug deep enough to capture an elephant.
But insects developed the same technique millions of
years ago. The larva of a spoon-winged lacewing
reminds us of the larval antlions (Myrmeleontidae)
that employ the same technique in warm countries
all over the world. A short-necked antlion (or
"doodlebug") uses its flat head to toss sand up the
slope when an ant starts sliding down. The predator
confuses its prey and gets its meal speedily. After
draining the nutritious juices from the victim, the
antlion flicks its head again and tosses the remains
away, clearing its trap for the next victim. H. C.
McCook tells of dropping three pebbles, all heavier
than the antlion, into the center of a pit where they
would be most inconvenient for its occupant. First
the antlion tried to toss out the pebbles. Failing in
this, the insect "placed the end of its abdomen
against and a little beneath a pebble and began to
push backward. A little time was taken to adjust the
pebble until its centre of gravity would be against the
end of the body. Then the animal began to back up
out of the pit. All of the three pebbles were thus
removed."
We can observe an antlion doing other unusual tricks.
When full-grown and ready to pupate, the insect
has a special way of keeping sand out of its pupal
chamber. First it spews a quick-setting silk from its
anal opening in a broad ring all around its body. Next
it completes the bottom of this mat and turns up the
edges to create a bowl. Grasping the structure firmly
and turning upside down with it, the antlion has one
half of its pupal cell in place. Swiveling skillfully, it
creates a second hemisphere under the first and joins
the two together. Not a grain is loose inside the
chamber. As might be guessed, the creature can
build a trap or construct a pupal cell in a bowlful of
granulated sugar or a dish of loose table salt. A bowl
of small glass beads will serve as well, so long as
insect prey can slip down the slope.
The adult antlion does not even have a common
name. It looks rather like a dragonfly but has short,
threadlike, knobbed antennae. When it settles on a
flower or leaf, it folds its four wings rooflike over its
long, slender abdomen as though it were a damselfly,
but with those telltale antennae thrust ahead. Unlike
a damselfly or a dragonfly, it is easy to catch between
thumb and forefinger; it is as though the insect knows
that its fastest flight would never be fast enough.

Owlflies (Ascalaphidae) show no such reluctance. By day, they launch themselves on four transparent wings—spanning two to four inches—and pursue smaller insects as prey. An owlfly drives its fore wings rapidly and lets the second pair trail. At rest, the creature seems even less like an owl. It wraps its wings around and below its body while raising its abdomen, turning it forward conspicuously above its back. Its long threadlike antennae, clubbed at the ends, may be pressed against the supporting branch and scarcely betray which is the insect's head end. Owlflies are mostly tropical, but we find a few in Europe, and in America as far north as New York State. Their larvae resemble antlions but dig no pits. Instead, they prowl through leaf litter in search of small insects.

A mantisfly (Mantispidae) is an even greater treasure because of its rarity, whether we discover it in the tropics, where most live, in Washington State, or even New York, where William T. Davis once found one of these creatures clinging to his jacket. The four wings of a mantisfly are clearly those of a neuropteran, covered with a multitude of veins and crossveins. But its inch-long body closely resembles that of a praying mantis, with forelegs elongated and modified for snatching prey. Like a true mantis, a mantisfly uses its slender middle and hind legs to leap upon a victim, usually a fly that has settled for a moment. The larval mantisfly resembles the immature stages of many carnivorous beetles. But if it can find the egg mass of a spider, it burrows in and changes form. As it feeds on the spider eggs, the mantisfly larva undergoes still further alterations, including two pupal stages in succession. A Brazilian mantisfly, *Symphasia varia*, has an equally unusual life history: its larvae live as parasites in the nest of a *Polybia* wasp. The adults of one mantisfly group, *Climaciella*, have several forms that almost precisely mimic paper wasps (*Polistes* sp.).

Even a freshwater sponge (*Spongilla*), bright green or gold and attached to a stick in a flowing stream, is not immune to attack from insects of this order. A spongillafly (Sisyridae) lays a cluster of eggs close to or at the water's edge. Thence, its larvae seek out a sponge and use their slender mouthparts to penetrate it as a food supply. When full-grown, they force their way through the surface film to pupate in a lacy, double-walled cocoon in leaf litter.

Along faster streams with many rapids, where the turbulent water brings air into solution, trout find quiet pools with abundant oxygen and there watch for insects to be brought to them by the current. Something edible is likely to lose its grip and be carried downstream to the waiting fish. This is the right place for an angler, and we meet many who have become expert judges of the aquatic insects that the trout eat. These fisherfolk in Canada and the northern United States know that the trout's greatest prize is a hellgrammite, also called a dobson, an arnly, a conniption-bug, a hell-devil, or a hell-diver. The insect may be almost three inches long, with a headful of muscles and powerful jaws, and about eight pairs of conspicuous filaments along the sides of its abdomen. Fishing enthusiasts favor it as bait because it will survive a day or two in a damp can and has a tough body wall that will hold a hook effectively. Hellgrammites that do not become a meal for a fish may crawl out of the water and find a place to pupate underground, beneath a stone or in a rotting log. At this stage, the creature will be at least three years old. In warm weather, the hellgrammite needs but another few weeks to transform into a wonderful Dobsonfly (*Corydalus cornutus*) with a wingspan of almost five inches. If the new adult is a female, her jaws will be short and strong and, like those of the larva, quite useful for self-defense. A male Dobsonfly is more spectacular because his slender, tapering jaws are an inch long, and more than adequate to hold a female while mating. His jaws may appear formidable, but he holds his mate quite gently.

A smaller version of the Dobsonfly, with miniature jaws, prowls for prey during its larval life among some of the same rapids where hellgrammites are found. The adult stage, which is known as a fishfly (*Chauliodes*), spends the day resting on the foliage or bark of some streamside tree. At night, like the Dobsonfly, a fishfly may be attracted to an artificial light. All of these insects bear translucent ash-gray wings with slightly darker veins. On a fishfly, the wings span about two inches.

If the soft wing of a fishfly or a Dobsonfly is held between thumb and forefinger, its flexible membranes top and bottom are felt as clearly separate in the open spaces among the meshwork of lengthwise veins and short crossveins. The wing is a great outward fold of the body wall, supported by its tubular veins. These veins provide space for fine nerves, air-filled branches of the respiratory system, and the slow flow of transparent blood that keeps the wing alive. Where the wing joins the body, small stiff areas and narrow lines of greater flexibility serve as a hinge. Short muscles inside the body oppose a general elasticity to furnish the motive power. They cause the wing to oscillate up and down and control the slight rotation on its long axis to gain better lift and propulsion.

We have no way of knowing whether the first winged insects on Earth had more control over their sallies into the air than does a Dobsonfly or fishfly on its fluttery airfoils today. Perhaps the remote ancestors could do no more than spread their wings and glide from a high place to a lower one, in the manner of a flying squirrel. Or possibly they jumped into space and fluttered their wings as frantically as a young wood duck does when it follows its mother out of its treehole nest; the wing action keeps the falling body from tumbling and lets the "flier" strike the ground belly-first for a safe landing.

At Cornell University, John Henry Comstock examined the wings of ancient and modern insects in minute detail. He hoped to discover more from these amazing organs than how they propel the insect through the air. He sought meaning in the fact that the hind wing of a Dobsonfly or a fishfly is broad at the base, with extra veins where it folds, fanlike, when the creature is at rest. No corresponding extra breadth and fanwise fold show on any lacewing, owlfly, mantisfly, or spongillafly: these are simply net-winged insects (Neuroptera).

The extra lobe does appear, like a marker of kinship, on the hind wings of alderflies (Sialidae), such as those that settled on alder trees near the shore of Thoreau's Walden Pond. On the bark of an alder or in the shade of a leaf, an alderfly becomes a solid shadow when it closes its broad, dark or smoky wings around its black body and against its support. In its few days as an adult, an alderfly (*Sialis*) follows the example of the Dobsonfly and fishfly in placing eggs where the hatchlings can enter fresh water. Usually the female finds a shallow where the somewhat flattened larva can seek weak prey in the mud of the bottom. Europeans have found larvae of alderflies prowling for food in sediment almost seventy feet below the water's surface, and their pupae in soil hundreds of yards from the nearest pond. No one knows how or why they go so far, or why the pupa lies on its side, as few insect pupae do.

A safe supposition, which the fossil record supports, is that alderflies, fishflies, and Dobsonflies represent a special branch among the net-winged insects. The Greek words for "ample wings" have been combined to give the group an order name of its own, the Megaloptera. Their ancestors may have been among the first to go through a pupal transformation. Such a change allows the adults with their floppy wings to be very different in form and behavior from their aquatic larvae. The insect-eater that the larvae must avoid is a trout or a pond fish; for the adult, a bat or bird is the main danger.

In the 18th century, the distinguished Swedish naturalist Carl von Linné (Carolus Linnaeus, as he is better known) classified among the net-winged insects he knew some quite dissimilar ones. These new additions to the order differed in having narrow oval wings, many veins, and crossveins; we now call them scorpionflies (Panorpidae). Members of this family are often encountered where they rest on a leaf in a sunny garden. The common name refers to the supposed resemblance between the enlarged end of a male scorpionfly's abdomen, which he curls up and forward above his back, and the scorpion's upturned tail with a swollen stinger at its tip. The male scorpionfly is harmless, and so is his mate, whose soft abdomen tapers to a point. Scorpionflies have long, downturned faces ending in small biting jaws. Their appearance, along with their long, threadlike antennae and long slender legs, combine to make the creature a unique neighbor in any forested part of the northern hemisphere.

Perhaps a scorpionfly's feeble flight limits its choice of food to items it can reach with a minimum of wing action. It devours any dead insect it can find, sips nectar occasionally, nibbles on ripe fruit, and even feeds on bird droppings. Its larva scavenges too, creeping like a caterpillar with extra prolegs to reach organic matter in moss or loose soil. Few of these foods have been available for the full 250 million years that scorpionflies have been around, essentially unchanged. Some of the now-extinct members of the order Mecoptera, to which the scorpionflies also belong, are suspected of being ancestors of the caddisflies (Trichoptera), the butterflies and moths (Lepidoptera), the true flies (Diptera), and probably the fleas (Siphonaptera) as well.

In France, R. Demoll found a scorpionfly capable of beating its wings fifty-six times per second and, from this knowledge, tried to calculate its flying speed. Never does one of these insects in our garden move faster than we can walk; nor can a male move fast enough to escape a hungry mate, for he routinely placates a female he finds by regurgitating a droplet of food from his crop as a gift. If she accepts and becomes diverted by the droplet, he can easily mate with her. Most of the scorpionflies we encounter have no mate to entertain them, and we see them just standing idly around.

A related family, the hangingflies (Bittacidae), show even greater patience. They prefer to eat fresh insect prey, yet they are unable to fly fast enough to catch anything. They solve this dilemma by letting themselves hang by their front feet from the edge of a projecting leaf or branch or even from a clothesline, while the four narrow wings are folded, concealing the abdomen, and the hind feet dangle inches below, in open air. Any flying insect that blunders into those hind feet gets caught. The hangingfly hauls up its victim and devours it, then lowers its legs to capture something else. Apparently the trick works often enough to keep hangingflies alert and active; they are found throughout the world. Each of these waiting insects could easily be mistaken for a crane fly, except that a hangingfly's antennae are long and threadlike, its face long like that of a scorpionfly, and its wings number four instead of two.

The snow scorpionfly (Boreidae) has given up flight altogether. Minute scales show where the wings should be on these tiny blackish or bronze insects, few of which grow to longer than 1/10 of an inch. The elongated face and the male's upturned tail help us to recognize them as they creep or leap about on the snowfields of the northern hemisphere. Perhaps the chill shortens our patience in observing them, for we have never seen a snow scorpionfly catch a meal. They must eat, however; perhaps they snatch unwary snow fleas (Collembola). Snow fleas flip themselves over the same snow, eating microscopic pollen grains dropped by the breeze or congregating on the sweet sap collecting in buckets hung from maple trees in early spring.

189. *A female dobsonfly (Corydalus sp.) on a lichen-covered rock is an easily overlooked touch of beauty in the Amazon jungle. Large, soft-bodied insects that fly mostly at night, dobsonflies are found along both slow- and fast-running streams, where their larval forms, commonly called hellgrammites, prey voraciously on aquatic insects. Dobsonflies have a wingspan of two to five inches, but they flutter about clumsily when airborne. Hellgrammites are a favorite bait of trout fishermen; if kept damp, they will live out of water for several days. Adult dobsonflies apparently do not feed; the males have huge mandibles that are used mainly to clasp the females during mating. Eggs are laid in masses of several thousand on rocks and on branches overhanging a stream.*
(Kjell B. Sandved)

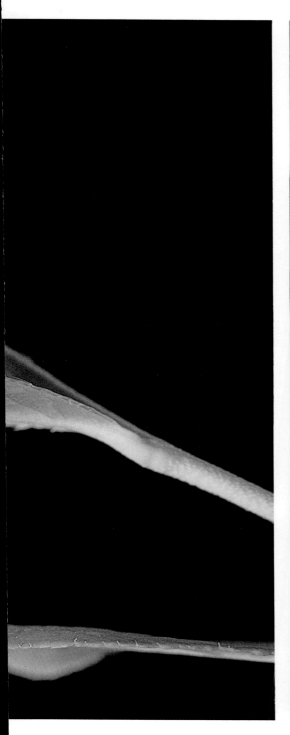

190. *Eggs of an eastern green lacewing,* Chrysopa ornata, *hang on slender silk stalks from the underside of a blueberry leaf in a Michigan meadow. Green lacewing larvae, with their piercing, sickle-shaped mandibles, are called "aphid-lions" because of their insatiable appetite for those tiny but destructive insects.* (Robert P. Carr)

191. *A hangingfly* (Bittacus *sp.*) *dangles from a leaf in a Michigan woodland, typically hanging on with its front and middle legs, leaving the raptorial hind feet free to grab small insects that fly past. Long, daggerlike mouthparts then bore a hole in the victim and suck out the body contents.* (Larry West)

192. *Close relatives of hangingflies, Wingless Scorpionflies (Apterobittacus apterus) are found in California grasslands, clinging to blades of grass and snagging prey with their hooklike hind feet. The larvae resemble spiny caterpillars and feed on dead insects and other organic matter in the duff.* (Edward S. Ross)

193 *top. Like the praying mantis which it resembles, the Styrian Mantisfly (Mantispa styriaca) of southern Europe has enlarged forelegs for grasping prey. This is not mimicry but an illustration of convergent evolution; two insects with widely different ancestries have adapted to similar ways of life. Larvae of these "false mantids" often develop in the egg sacs of large spiders.* (Hervé Chaumeton/Jacana)

193 *bottom. A finely tuned killing machine, this common scorpionfly (Panorpa sp.) could itself become the sudden victim of a dragonfly, robber fly, spider, or insect-eating bird. The name "scorpionfly" derives from the male's bulbous (but harmless) genitalia, which curve upward over the abdomen like the stinger of a scorpion.* (Pierre Pilloud/Jacana)

194 *overleaf. Snow scorpionflies (Boreus sp.) copulate on the thawing winter blanket of a Michigan woodland. One-eighth of an inch long, snow scorpionflies live in patches of moss in cold northern forests, feeding on springtails, small insects, and on the moss itself. Their black color absorbs heat when they emerge on warm winter days to hop across the snow cover. Snow scorpionflies are flightless; the male has bristlelike wings to hold the female during mating.* (Larry West)

196. *A raft of more than a hundred* Culex *mosquito eggs drifts between islands of duckweed in a Maine pond, kept afloat by air trapped in interstices between the eggs. In a few days the larvae will enter the water by popping caps off the lower ends of the eggs. If the female* Culex *drinks blood before laying eggs, her raft may contain several hundred eggs. In contrast, eggs of malaria-carrying* Anopheles *mosquitoes are laid singly on the surface of the water, each eggshell kept afloat by a rim of air pockets. And many kinds of mosquitoes have no way to float their eggs; for example,* Aedes *mosquitoes lay their eggs in dry depressions that will be flooded in spring.* (Dwight R. Kuhn)

Two-winged Aviators

The first person to discover what makes an insect a fly was Aristotle. It was he who recognized that the possession of just one pair of wings was the most distinctive feature among the flies of the world. Combining the Greek words for *two* and *wings*, he produced the word *Diptera* as the ideal group name for flies. The single pair of wings in flies corresponds to the fore wings of insects with two pairs. The second pair of wings is modified to appear as two tiny, knob-ended organs called halteres. Vibrations of the halteres stabilize the body in flight.

Energetic creatures that beat their wings 300 to 2,000 times a second, or more slowly in courtship gestures, flies have become firmly established on our planet. The Diptera make up the fourth largest order of insects, with more than 86,000 species known worldwide, and about 16,300 in North America. Just a few seem to have lost the ability to fly, after taking up residence on remote oceanic islands, on mountain peaks, in caves or loose soil, or as external parasites on larger animals. In all of these situations, flight and wings may be handicaps. But elsewhere they are immense advantages.

While still immature, most flies depend upon liquid food or substances that can be liquefied and sucked in. Their adult mouthparts are varied, extremely versatile, mostly adapted to sucking, piercing, or lapping liquid nourishment that can be swallowed easily. These habits promote contamination with bacteria and other agents of disease, giving flies a bad name. Nonetheless, their ability to gain easy access to liquid food and to depart with it quickly on just two wings contributes mightily to making flies so very diverse and numerous.

A fly that stands still on a daisy, with its wings outstretched as it sips nectar from one floret after another, may have a fuzzy enough body to merit the name "bee fly" (Bombyliidae). Examination reveals its similarity to a monoplane. The torpedo-shaped fuselage and back-swept dihedral of the wings are behind a rounded anterior end where great, curved compound eyes take the place of windows in an airplane cockpit. Each eye is a complex array of a thousand facets, every one of them facing in a slightly different direction and reporting to the insect the amount of light it sees. This information gives the fly no really clear picture of its world, but is most effective in reporting any change that indicates movement nearby. The approach of an insect-eater, or any threatening gesture, causes the insect to depart at once. It leaps into the air, vibrating its wings, and either hovers to get another look (as any bee fly can) or dashes elsewhere for safety. The bee fly combines vision with scent to recognize a real bee or a wasp that comes to the same flower, then follows the other insect to its nest, where the bee fly lays an egg. There, a maggot from a bee fly egg will have a food supply ready made.

Still bigger eyes and better vision allow a robber fly of the family Asilidae to choose which insect to attack; nourishment is then taken through a beaklike extension of the head that the robber fly forces into the body of its victim. When the same technique is applied to us, as we walk along some woodland path or over an open beach, the attacker is usually a horse fly or a deer fly (Tabanidae). Its bulging eyes often meet on the midline above and alert the insect to anything that moves and might have a blood meal to offer. The stab wound is far more painful than the "bite" of any mosquito (Culicidae) or black fly (Simuliidae). These insects employ more subtle cues: the warmth of a living body and the carbon dioxide exhaled by suitable victims. People differ more than they realize in their output of heat and consequently in their attractiveness to these and other blood-sucking insects.

We take scant comfort from knowing that only female mosquitoes and black flies want our blood. Their mates are elsewhere, feeding only on dew, nectar, and plant juices. Counterparts of the sharp stylets with which the female stabs so deeply let the male sip the liquids he wants. The female cannot be so easily satisfied, for she needs the protein in blood to produce her full quota of eggs. Without a blood meal she can lay very few, and then only by digesting some of the muscles that drive her wings and thereby grounding herself forever.

A female mosquito ordinarily lives long enough as an adult to meet a mate and to sample the blood from several victims in slow succession. This gives time for an infection that is picked up from an earlier victim to propagate inside her body and make her an effective transmitter of disease to a later victim. Malaria organisms are disseminated this way as they ride along in an *Anopheles* mosquito. We have almost forgotten that this disease used to be a hazard for people living well beyond the tropics, in cities as far north as Boston and Moscow. The epidemics ceased before anyone discovered the role of *Anopheles* in carrying the infection. Changes in urban drainage removed the breeding places of the mosquitoes, while newer modes of construction decreased the access of mosquitoes to housing. Now people can dream of eliminating malaria worldwide.

The hairy, segmented antennae on a female mosquito, and the feathery ones on her mate, remind us that these insects and their kin in some other families are among the oldest types of flies on Earth. Their ancestors may have found thin places in the skin of dinosaurs as sites for sipping blood. These old-style flies have larvae that show some indication of a head, with jaws and, sometimes, compound eyes. The wriggler stages of mosquitoes, the wormlike young of midges (Chironomidae), and the so-called "leather-jacket" larvae of crane flies (Tipulidae) are familiar representatives. When fully grown, these larvae form a naked pupa, on the outside of which the legs and body parts of the pre-emergent adult-to-be can be readily distinguished.

Midge larvae of one common worldwide genus, *Chironomus*, have become important indicators of extreme pollution in stream and lake water. Known as "blood worms" because of their bright red color, they scavenge in the bottom muck where bacteria have already used up all the dissolved oxygen. So long as the blood worms can find plenty of organic matter to eat, they can suspend normal respiration. The adults into which they grow are harmless midges that we see dancing in the air above bushes and trees. Sometimes they choose to dance right after sunset, when warm air is still rising above a paved road heated by the sun.

Rotting vegetable matter or the fungus that grows on it attracts fungus gnats (Mycetophilidae); they are even drawn to a flower pot on a windowsill. Countless numbers of these small, slim, soft-bodied flies with feathery antennae roam through forests, woodlands, stream margins, and other humid habitats outdoors. Perhaps some of the larvae feed on other insects that are there. The predatory larvae of a large fungus gnat, *Arachnocampa luminosa*, are famous in New Zealand as the "glowworms" of the Waitomo Caves. Each luminous, translucent larva suspends itself in a hammock of slime close to the grotto roof, and there secretes multiple dangling threads with sticky globules, forming a beaded curtain with which to capture small flying insects as prey. We joined other visitors floating in a small boat on the river that flows through Waitomo and gazed awestruck at the constellation of glowworms shining in the darkness close overhead. All the food these insects need for a lifetime is gained during their larval stages; the adults partake of little more than dew. We found glowworms in many places outdoors on both large islands of New Zealand, wherever they could find a relatively wind-free situation in which to hang their sticky curtains. A fist-sized pocket in the side of a road cut and a space under a tree root where erosion had carried away the soil were both large enough to accommodate a glowworm and add interest to a nocturnal field trip as soon as our flashlight was turned off.

A completely different way to make a living has been perfected by the gall gnats (Cecidomyidae) and some of the spotted-winged fruit flies or peacock flies (Tephritidae). Many of them simply leave an egg on a suitable stem or leaf. The maggot bores in and eats out a home in the central tissues, but releases a chemical that stimulates the plant to produce more edible cells locally. It is on these cells that the maggot feeds. The remainder of the plant may grow normally, or the presence of the invader may show externally as a swelling of the stem or a wartlike projection from a leaf; each such disfigurement is called a gall. Usually, the inherited behavior of the maggot includes one final act prior to pupation: the preparation of an exit tunnel from the central feeding chamber to, but not through, the thin epidermis. The emerging fly must be able to force its way through the epidermal seal to reach the outside world, there to expand its wings, fly in search of a mate, and ensure the propagation of its species. Some of these little maggots tunnel through a thin leaf between the upper and lower epidermis layers, destroying tissue that the plant cannot replace. We notice most often those that skeletonize the foliage of white birches in New England, almost depriving the trees of the means to make food with sunlight before the growing season is finished.

Almost every kind of plant material that contains nourishment is exploited by fly maggots of some kind. Seaweed flies (Coelopidae) lay their eggs on coarse, dying seaweeds cast up on shore by storm waves. Rather similar flies are encountered as much as 15,000 feet above sea level on the slopes of the Himalayas, where pollen grains blown from lower elevations provide the sole known source of nourishment for the frost-resistant maggots. At more modest altitudes, flies and their maggots tidy up the earth, recycling wastes and dead bodies while gaining a little food for themselves. Seen as adults at close range, many have a beauty we might not anticipate from their lowly role. Even the little Pomace Fly (*Drosophila melanogaster*), which has proven to be so helpful in the study of heredity, stays bright and clean as it frequents apple pulp from which cider has been squeezed or overripe, fermenting fruit. A pair of these little flies can beget two hundred or more offspring in less than two weeks almost anywhere on Earth. Hawaii has the greatest diversity of them in the world.

Among the many families of flies, a progression can be traced from the primitive midges and mosquitoes, crane flies, and fungus gnats, to insects of more compact body design and more regular development. The offspring of flies in the latter group tend to be more numerous, their maggots simpler— without eyes or jaws. They pupate within their last larval skin, which reveals nothing of the adult fly until it breaks open a circular cap at one end and emerges to spread its wings. The adult's antennae are short, with no more than three segments, and usually with a prominent bristle projecting forward. We can think of the more compact, modern flies as

201

coming into existence along with flowering plants. Such flies formed only a minor part of the fauna at the time the Baltic amber was being formed. Few are represented in the fossilized gum. Yet today these are the flies we meet most often. Many sip nectar from flowers, unwittingly accomplishing cross-pollination. The most spectacular aerialists among them are the hover flies of the family Syrphidae. When approached, a hover fly leaps into the air, vibrating its wings skillfully to maintain its position in space like a helicopter. It can dart quickly in almost any direction to escape a perceived danger. Some hover flies use their superb flying abilities in a life history similar to that of the bee flies. They follow bees and wasps from flower to nest, there dropping eggs from which maggots emerge to feast on the young of the bees or wasps. Other hover flies place their eggs on foliage near infestations of aphids, and their maggots—often strikingly colorful—prey on these soft-bodied sap-suckers. If the aphids are on a valuable plant, we think of the hover fly as a friend, and protect it in any way we can.

One hover fly so closely resembles a Honeybee in size, coloration, flower-visiting habits, and buzzing sounds that it is called the Drone Fly (*Eristalis tenax*) in North America and Europe. If it finds daisies and other suitable flowers to visit in a small garden, it may remain there for weeks. To reproduce it may seek a tree hole, where wet rotting wood gives off an attractive scent; privies and the decaying flesh of a large dead animal are other favorite spots. There the larvae can rummage about for food in decaying matter while extending a telescoping "tail" like a snorkel into the air above any standing liquid two inches deep or less. This "rat-tailed maggot" and the adult Drone Flies may well have been the real basis for the Biblical story of the "bees" in a dead lion (*Judges* 14, 5–14). The claim that honey was obtained at the site would be inconsistent with this view, but the story is equally improbable from a knowledge of the actual habits of Honeybees.

A more common visitor we find at a large dead animal is a flesh fly (Calliphoridae), usually a female that has eggs to drop or newly hatched maggots to leave. She will deposit these on any dead vertebrate or even on an open wound that is left unprotected. During World War I, medical technicians discovered that flesh fly maggots will clean up torn tissues without attacking healthy human cells, introducing no infection and actually helping a wound to begin its normal healing process.

The habits of a flesh fly seem only a step removed from those of bot flies (Oestridae), whose maggots make themselves at home until they are full grown in a hair follicle or some similar inpocketing of skin where the mammal must supply nourishment. The grown larva leaves its host to pupate in the soil and emerge as an adult, prepared to mate and repeat the process. A friend of ours who had long experience in the American tropics had the fortitude to let a Human Bot Fly (*Dermatobia hominis*) complete its development in a painful ulcer on his forearm, all to capture the insect as it emerged and have an adult Human Bot Fly for his collection.

People should appreciate far more the behavior of tachina flies (Tachinidae), which seek out caterpillars and other insects as hiding places for their eggs. Upon hatching, the maggots burrow into the victim and devour it from inside. Fat-storage centers are eaten first; last to be attacked are organs that are essential for the survival of the insect host. When the victim dies, the tachina maggot should be able to feast briefly on the remains, then transform into an adult fly. So specific are the host preferences of these destructive parasites that they can often be moved from a country or continent to which a pest insect is native, and continue their operations on this species alone in a fresh location. Once it has been suitably situated, the parasite adjusts to any minor changes in its host. The victim, which may be attacking a crop of importance to people, cannot become immune, as it might to some chemical formulation introduced into its environment as a pesticide.

So far, no natural control has been found to reduce populations of the House Fly (*Musca domestica*), which has become worldwide through its ability to reproduce rapidly in the wastes of domestic animals. Wherever humankind has introduced horses and cattle, the House Fly has gone along. Its eggs and maggots develop in rotting manure, aided by warmth produced by decomposition. Only where manure is spread thin on fields are birds likely to eat the maggots before they can pupate.

The slightly smaller Biting Stable Fly (*Stomoxys calcitrans*) often attacks people resting on a beach. Its larval stages develop in decaying vegetation; both sexes live on blood meals and possess stilettolike, forward-directed mouthparts. The armament is easy to notice, and quite dissimilar to the blunt sponging pad below a House Fly's head. The Biting Stable Fly seems not even to wait a moment before stabbing in, whereas a House Fly ordinarily walks about a little, tasting its support through mouthparts and sensitive front feet, attempting to learn where the richest food is to be found.

Everyone in the Americas and Eurasia should be glad that these areas do not have a representative of a more distantly related group of bloodsuckers, the tsetse flies (*Glossina* spp.) of Africa. After mating, a female tsetse hunts at a moderate pace while inside her a single egg releases a maggot; that maggot grows, with food supplied, inside its mother. Not until fully developed and ready to pupate will the maggot come out. It drops to the ground, burrows in, and transforms, while another maggot is already developing inside the mother. She continues to live, to feed at intervals on blood from animals of many kinds (reptiles, birds, mammals, people), and to transfer the infective agents that cause the deadly disease *nagana* in livestock and sleeping sickness in humankind. The prevalence of tsetse flies and of the disease, which causes almost no symptoms in the native animals attacked by the fly, has long closed major areas of Africa to successful ranching and human settlement. No way has been found yet to eliminate the fly or the disease, despite heroic efforts in both directions.

205. *In a cave in central Mexico, the transparent larvae of fungus gnats (family Mycetophilidae) exude sticky curtains to trap flying insects. In a windless environment, the strands may be several feet long. The larvae of only a few species of fungus gnats are predatory; most, as their common and scientific names suggest, live on fungi, mold, and decaying plant material in dark, damp places. A mushroom riddled with holes is the work of a Mycetophila grub. The short-lived adults are sometimes seen indoors and mistaken for mosquitoes.* (Robert W. Mitchell)

206 *overleaf. Crane flies (family Tipulidae) cling to the strands of a spider web in an Angolan forest, the touch of their long, slender legs too light to arouse an attack by the predatory arachnid. Resembling giant mosquitoes, crane flies number many thousands of species worldwide, some having wingspans of more than three inches. They often stray indoors, startling people who are unaware that the slow-flying crane fly cannot bite and is harmless. If seized by a predator, the fragile legs easily break off, allowing the crane fly to escape otherwise unharmed.* (Edward S. Ross)

208. *These bulging, brightly colored eyes and menacing beak belong to a horse fly (family Tabanidae), an inch-long pest as nasty as its portrait suggests. Silent in motion, the female horse fly lands unnoticed, delivering a painful bite with knifelike mouthparts as she sucks blood. An anticoagulant in the fly's saliva causes the wound to bleed for several minutes. Livestock attacked by horse flies can become weak from loss of blood, and the lesions invite screwworm infestation. Male horse flies are mild-mannered, feeding on pollen and nectar. Males are seldom noticed by people, and live only long enough to mate.* (Charles Krebs)

209 *top and bottom. Fast-flying robber flies (family Asilidae) pounce on their unsuspecting prey from above, seizing the victim with long spiny legs, sucking its body dry, and discarding the remains in a heap below a favorite perch. Robber flies rival dragonflies in their skills as aerial hunters, preying on other flies, bees, leafhoppers, grasshoppers, butterflies, moths—even on dragonflies themselves. Some species specialize in hunting Honeybees, waiting like tiny falcons on twigs with a clear view of flowers where the bees are feeding. Other robber flies mimic bumblebees perfectly, a protection against other predators who fear being stung.* (top Edward S. Ross; bottom C. A. Latch/Marcon Photo)

210 *overleaf. A Drone Fly* (Eristalis tenax) *visits a rhododendron in a North Carolina garden. Named for its resemblance to the Honeybee, the Drone Fly is among the most common insects across the Northern Hemisphere. However, entomologists believe it was unknown in the New World until the 1600s, its larvae crossing the Atlantic in ships carrying colonists from Europe—perhaps the* Mayflower *itself. Drone Fly larvae thrive in polluted water, breathing through a long tube that has given them the name "rat-tailed maggots."* (Edward S. Ross)

212. *At a nest of the European Hornet (Vespa crabro) in southern France, workers clean empty cells while larvae seal themselves into cells prior to pupating. Introduced more than a century ago to North America, where it is known as the Giant Hornet, this inch-long brown-and-yellow wasp constructs its paper-covered nests in hollow trees, beneath porches, and in outbuildings, using plant materials chewed into a pulp. The fertilized queen spends the winter in hibernation, emerging in spring to found a new colony. She will feed the first larvae, regurgitating bits of insect prey, until the young develop into female workers who will tend subsequent generations of workers, plus fertile males and females. The entire colony, except for new queens, dies in the fall, having produced as many as 25,000 individuals since spring. (René Pierre Bille)*

Builders and Architects

The social insects are often recommended as models of selfless dedication and peaceful cooperation, or as ideal examples of interaction for humankind to emulate. "Go to the ant, thou sluggard: consider her ways, and be wise," the Bible tells us. Yet we can scarcely think of just a single ant, or termite, or Honeybee. These insects show an endless tolerance of, or an actual need for, association in groups. They always live together in colonies. And seldom does a group consist of fewer than a hundred individuals, or include any members except the short-lived progeny of an original long-lived female, the one we choose to call the queen.

The queen begins construction of a nest to provide climate control and shelter for her developing young. As successive broods mature, all of them "workers" or nonreproductive individuals, the queen relinquishes to them the labor of nest building and brood care. They tend to their mother, the queen, and free her of all duties except egg-laying. Their uniform heritage almost guarantees cooperation in the growing family, and a continuation of its pattern of architecture. The queen's way will be theirs too, as long as the colony survives.

Chemical messages that originate with the queen coordinate the colony, inducing consistent behavior among members as they attend to its protection, nutrition, and reproduction. William Morton Wheeler at Harvard University recognized the resemblance of the colony to a single organism. In 1911, he described an insect colony as "a complex, definitely coordinated and therefore individualistic system of activities, which are primarily directed to obtaining and assimilating substances from the environment, to producing other similar systems, known as offspring, and to protecting the system itself and usually also its offspring from disturbances emanating from the environment." The Belgian playwright Maurice Maeterlinck expressed the same thought in his rather mystical account, *The Life of the Termites* (1926), noting that the individual insects were as mortal as the individual cells in a person, but the community of them carried on. A colony was *un seul être vivant*, a single living entity.

Near Cape Town in South Africa, we listened to S. H. Skaife as he shared with us his admiration for the termites he had been studying throughout the course of his lifetime. "Of course they engage in cannibalism, eating excess brothers and sisters, when this action will aid the social economy. And the secondary reproductives, male and female, in remote corners of the nest engage in incest to contribute more fertilized eggs for the good of the local population. But do the termites let anything get out of hand? Unlike ants, they engage in no slave-making, almost no theft or parasitism." He had a colony of the Black-mound Termite (*Amitermes atlanticus*), whose members he kept under close observation on a metal-clad table in his living room. They did not spread elsewhere in the house or need anything other than the dry grain and grasses he set out for them. His only complaint was that the termites dwell in darkness.

Elsewhere we hear mostly about the damage termites do to wooden houses, furniture and books. Destruction of human handiwork, particularly in the tropics, where termites are quite numerous and widespread, is rapid and severe; abandoned wooden dwellings often disappear completely. Tropical termites recycle dead wood rapidly, releasing its nutrients for absorption by living roots. They contribute immensely to the abundance of tropical life, both plant and animal.

Only in Australia can we meet the most primitive termites, *Mastotermes*. The insects do not confine themselves to wood-eating or to constructing galleries in fallen trees and stumps. Often they eat out the heartwood from living eucalyptus trees and, on occasion, do serious damage to healthy fruit trees and vegetable crops.

Most termite societies behave in ways that appear eminently logical. To nest in a tree close to a reliable supply of wood makes special sense in the American tropics, where the annual rainfall of over ninety inches is well distributed through the year. Galleries dug underground would be in danger of flooding both day and night. Some termites will take chances by building outside their tree a "carton nest," like papier-mâché, made from wood fibers cemented together with glutinous saliva or feces. Some carton nests form conspicuous masses partway up a tree trunk. Others spread diffusely along branches as slender tubes through which the termites can run unseen from place to place. Still others resemble massive apartment houses the shape of a football on some sturdy branch, with dozens of inner layers as well as thousands of interconnected, labyrinthine passageways.

A carton nest is too weak to resist the beak of a big woodpecker or the curved claws of a powerful anteater clambering in the tree. To combat persistent ants or other invading insects, the termites maintain an internal security force. Some of the workers in the colony show great development in a gland that opens through a forward-directed nozzle on the head. Called nasutes, these specially-equipped insects station themselves at strategic points in the galleries and are fed there by other workers. Nasutes stay ready to squirt their repellent secretion—mostly concentrated formic acid—on any invader. Whenever we have used a pocket knife to open a small window in the side of a carton nest and see the termites in the galleries, nasutes by the dozen have arrived in seconds with weapons ready. Anything that moves becomes their target.

Where flooding is a rare hazard, termites of other species dig galleries underground and travel unseen to sources of wood fiber or to hunting grounds from which they emerge at night to forage for vegetable matter. Some reveal the location of their hidden passages by constructing vertical tubes to and above the soil surface, thereby ventilating the underground chambers. Frequently, their passageways are works of art, with multiple walls perforated by minute holes that permit air exchange.

Termite nests that extend above ground are almost cement-hard, composed of mineral particles held together with saliva and feces. These strange features of the landscape, up to twenty feet tall, occur in most semiarid parts of Africa, Asia, Central and South America, and Australia. In each termite mound, a large central chamber, at or below ground level, houses the original queen and her consort. She may have grown to the size of a human finger, with an enormous abdomen distended by developing eggs. This awkward body shape keeps her from moving about, effectively imprisoning her for life. Workers and fresh air reach the royal pair through radiating passageways. Channels for air-conditioning permit warmth to rise inside the dome of the mound, then convey it down through ducts close to the surface of the side walls. There it escapes, while oxygen from the atmosphere diffuses in to take the place of carbon dioxide. Thence the gas returns to the royal chamber, cooled and freshened, only to rise on another circuit.

Near Darwin in northern Australia, the Compass Termite (*Omitermes meridionalis*) produces mounds remarkable because they are invariably oriented along a north-south axis. These mounds may be as much as twelve feet high, and stretch ten feet from north to south, but are seldom more than three feet thick. The construction plan allows the mound to turn one broad face to the morning sun while keeping the other shaded. By midday, the mound casts almost no shadow and absorbs a minimum of solar energy. All afternoon the second side receives the sun and the first is shaded. Maintaining a gradient of temperature inside the mound lets the termites use the heat to best effect.

Such an array of mounds may suggest a city of skyscrapers and permanence. Yet each mound is dynamic. If damaged, it is repaired in a day or two. New mounds rise up in a similarly short time, then are enlarged without the termites ever showing themselves. Such mounds often endanger landings on airstrips in the Australian outback. A bulldozer may be called in to flatten the mounds, but the efforts of the hard-working termites make the confrontations almost endless.

Certain termites in Africa, like certain ants in warm parts of the New World, have become quite skilled agriculturalists. They use their nests as protected places in which to raise fungus plants under exquisite control. The termites begin their enterprise in special chambers within the nest, accumulating their own excrement and mixing it with vegetable fragments collected in the open at night. To the mixture in each new nest, the new termite queen brings a pellet of fungus as a starter, which she carried from her earlier home. She inserts the pellet into the mass of excrement, and fungus grows quickly over the food supply, which may originally be the size of a human fist. Soon it produces "ambrosia bodies," tiny knobs of fungus smaller than poppy seeds. Young termites often settle on the fungus garden and repeatedly eat their fill of ambrosia bodies. Adults visit less often, but they carry off ambrosia bodies to share with the queen and her consort, and with other termites farther from the common supply.

Each community of fungus-growing termites recycles bits of vegetation faster than could occur without such efforts. Members of a large colony may haul home and process half a ton of plant material annually. They vary their routine only when the rainy season begins. They then begin housecleaning and dismantle the fungus garden completely. They spread every crumb of it on the ground outside, close to the nest mound. The fungus strands join up and raise a whole crop of mushrooms. The breeze carries away most of the microscopic spores, but some drop to the ground. Termites rake up soil beneath the mushrooms and take it to their renovated chamber. From this, fungus spreads to fresh compost and renews the termites' food supply.

The ants with a similar dietary preference are the leaf-cutters (*Atta* spp.) of tropical America. We discover their well-traveled trails, about four inches wide and hundreds of yards long, from the nest doorway to the forest edge. There the ants climb to foliage that attracts them, using their jaws like razor blades to cut a fragment half an inch across, and dexterously swing it overhead like a green sail clamped firmly in their jaws. Climbing down to the nearest path with the trophies, they head for home. Once inside their nest, the leaf-cutters get help from other workers to press the leaf fragments into a decaying mass of vegetation—a real compost heap. They then coat each fragment with a drop of excrement as fertilizer. Fungus spreads over the underground mass, often in chambers the size of a bushel basket. Nourishment in the leaf fragments is transformed into tiny gray knobs of fungus that the ants eat. It is their only known food.

Usually the leaf-cutters use the earth they excavate to build a high ridge as a dike around the nest opening. The wall protects their nest by deflecting any runoff water in a storm. Yet no ants build mounds as formidable as those of tropical termites, nor do they renew their "hills" so promptly after a mound is wrecked.

Most underground ant nests bulge upward only to the degree that excavated material is spread around the doorways at the surface. Out of sight, the walls of each passageway through the soil are smoothed by the ants, then moistened with saliva, which hardens the soil and thereby reduces the chance of cave-ins. Often the ants incorporate the roots and growing stems of plants into their earthen nests in moist soil, which provide reinforcement and support. One such mound of the Field Ant (*Formica exsectoides*) that we have been visiting for more than a decade is about four feet across and a foot high, firmly grassed over and solid enough to stand on. A mound three times as wide, built by Wood Ants (*Formica rufa*) in Europe, has been maintained for fifteen years without any perceptible change—photographic records of it have been kept throughout this period. Such a colony may consist of as many as half a million individuals, all working for the common good and coordinated in their efforts by chemical exudates transferred to them from their queen.

Far fewer adults and young can be accommodated in the small natural cavities that some ants colonize. The space may be an empty snail shell or a gap in a plant, perhaps where the stalk of a leaf joins the stem. *Azteca* ants of the American tropics gain entry into hollows in the stems of cecropias—a common pioneer tree in clearings. In Africa and elsewhere we meet *Crematogaster* ants, which cut access doorways into the hollow thorns on shrubby acacias. If we jostle the shrub or tree, the ants rush out, biting and stinging as though to protect the plant from a major attack.

Bees and wasps create nests that are not as gigantic or conspicuous. The shelter in which their young develop may be a small burrow or perhaps a cavity excavated within the broken stem of a plant. All over the world, leaf-cutter bees (*Megachile* spp.) line their stem cavities with crescent-shaped pieces cut from leaves or petals. The same material is used to isolate one cell from the next in the assembly line. After stocking each cell with pollen and a little honey, the parent adds a single egg and closes up the door. The food supply left by the mother must suffice for her maggotlike larva until it transforms into an adult and leaves its cell. Whichever youngster is in the cell at the end of the line must complete its growth and emerge before the next in line can break out and escape through the vacated cell. This frees the next in line and so on until all are free.

Easier to observe are the private escape routes that mother wasps provide as they build their nests. A mud-dauber wasp, such as *Sceliphron caementarium* in America, a Cicada-killer Wasp (*Sphecius speciosus*) in the New World, and a sand wasp (*Bembix*) in America or Eurasia still prepare an individual nest cell first, then go hunting for food with which to stock it. The mud-dauber brings back spiders, each one immobilized with venom from the stinger. The Cicada-killer hunts for cicadas—a single large one or two smaller ones—for a nest cell. The sand wasp larva hatches in the cell beside a fly that the parent has left as food; the mother returns repeatedly with more flies, opening the door to restock her larva's pantry. Paper wasps (*Polistes* spp.) of the North Temperate Zone and hornets (*Vespa* or *Vespula* spp.) are among those that return to feed chewed-up insects to their young in the brood cells. Paper wasps feed their young from the top of their vertical cells, hornets from the bottom. Eventually the mothers and workers can rest while the larvae pupate. Wherever frost is frequent or severe, only young mated females survive the winter.

We note something similar among bees. In spring, large mated female bumblebees (*Bombus* spp.) in the Americas or Eurasia emerge from their winter sleep to hunt for a hole, such as an abandoned chipmunk burrow. There each bee builds a waxy honeypot and a brood cell close by. After filling the honeypot, the bee lays an egg in her brood cell. She stays close, sipping from her food supply and contributing some body heat to her egg, and eventually to her larva, hastening its development. She feeds her larva until it grows enough to pupate. Her offspring will be smaller than she is, but each newly-matured bee helps to raise new generations during the summer. The last young of the year must eat especially well and gain the fullest possible size, with an inner store of nourishment for the winter.

Honeybees (*Apis mellifera*) carry temperature control to an extreme. All winter long, the nonreproductive workers cluster around their queen and keep her warm. They restore their own energy at intervals by snacking from the honey store. A colony of 50,000 bees may need fifty pounds of honey to supply them through the winter; they need good insulation from the wind as well, and often seek shelter inside a hollow tree or a man-made hive.

When spring arrives, the worker Honeybees fly forth to gather more nectar and pollen. The queen resumes her egg-laying, depositing one egg in each cell of the brood comb after some recently emerged worker has swabbed the inside of the cell with her tongue. Slightly older workers will feed the larvae in the brood comb until each grows enough to be closed in and pupate. Everything in the hive proceeds according to an inherited program. Thirteen to fourteen days after a new worker emerges from her natal cell, she will produce wax on the underside of her abdomen. Inner guidance will direct her to use the wax to construct six-sided cells of either brood comb or honeycomb, according to the colony's needs. She will continue shaping the wax until her supply runs out, then go off to other duties. Slightly younger workers will fill in where she left off, each acting on its own, never two together.

Honeybee bodies, so uniform in size, provide the measuring system that keeps the comb so regular. Third-century mathematician Pappus the Alexandrine suggested that bees build in this way to economize with wax and prove themselves endowed "with a certain geometrical forethought." Now we know better. As the crystallographer Erasmus Bartholin judged in the 17th century, each bee strives to make a new cell as large as possible, and squeezes against adjacent cells in the construction process. We marvel at the myriad ways in which these social insects, less than an inch in length, regulate the inner perfection of the hive.

221. *A female paper wasp* (Polistes sp.) *works on a nest attached to the fan of a Florida palmetto. The small nests of paper wasps, built of a fast-hardening mass of pulp and saliva by a team of several females, consist of single, circular combs with uncovered hexagonal cells. In a paper wasp society, the female who began the nest-building dominates her workmates once the comb is completed. She will eat their eggs, and once they have tended the first generation of her larvae, they will be driven away. Most paper wasps are less belligerent than hornets and yellow jackets, but all three can deliver a painful sting.* (John Shaw)

222 *overleaf. True to their reputation,* Honeybees (Apis mellifera) *busy about a hive in Idaho. There is one species of domesticated Honeybee worldwide, although certain races are more popular with bee-keepers because of their gentle manner. Brought to North America in the early 17th century, Honeybees today pollinate eighty percent of the commercial crops in the United States. It is particularly vulnerable to certain pesticides, and bee populations vital to fruit-growers have been devastated by ill-conceived spraying programs. Life in a Honeybee colony centers on the queen, who will produce hundreds of eggs daily over a lifetime of several years, mating on the wing with large-eyed drones who are killed after insemination takes place. The hive is maintained by thousands of workers, who produce honey and feed their queen and the larvae.* (Jeffrey Foott)

224 *overleaf. The honey filling the cells of this comb will have a distinctive flavor, for worker* Honeybees *from a colony visit a single kind of flower until they have exhausted its supply of nectar and pollen. Clover honey is a mainstay of the $50 million honey market in the United States, but very special taste treats are to be found among many regional favorites, notably orange-blossom honey from Florida, blueberry honey from Maine, and sage honey from Utah.* (Jeffrey Foott)

224

226. *Heavy, dripping combs from a wild Honeybee hive bulge from the crevice of an old oak tree in Wisconsin. Such bee trees, containing as much as three hundred pounds of honey, are prized by country folk and black bears. In 1839, the neighboring states of Missouri and Iowa nearly went to war over disputed ownership of 2,600 square miles of land rich in bee trees. Oldtime honey-hunters developed elaborate tricks to find wild bee colonies, luring the worker bees to sweet bait, marking their line of flight, and following it to the hive.*
(Stephen J. Krasemann/DRK Photo)

227. *A Yellow Bumblebee (Bombus fervidus) rests for the night on a marigold blossom in a Michigan garden. Bumblebees nest on or in the ground, often choosing old mouse nests and animal burrows. Beginning with just a single hibernating female, a colony may number several hundred individuals by autumn. Bumblebees are important pollinators of red clover, for other species do not have a tongue long enough to reach the nectar in the flower's deep corolla.* (John Shaw)

230 *overleaf. A harvester ant (Veromesser sp.) carries the bud from a mallow plant to its nest in the Sonoran Desert of Arizona. Harvester ants collect and husk seeds for use in winter or drought. But they are often seen bearing buds, flowers, and feathers in their strong mandibles. If their nest is disturbed, the fleeing ants will carry these seemingly useless treasures with them. In North Africa, the granaries of harvester ant colonies have been found to contain several hundred pounds of seeds.* (Jeffrey Foott)

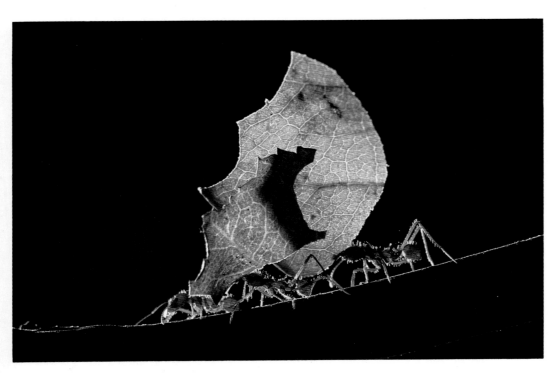

228 and **229.** *Leaf-cutter ants (Atta sp.) harvest pieces of foliage not for food but as compost. Carried to the nest like green parasols, the fragments are chewed into fertilizer for a fungus garden that feeds the entire colony. Leaf-cutter ants are found in Texas, Louisiana, and Central and South America. Different leaf-cutters have different harvesting techniques.*

Workers may climb a tree and drop pieces of leaves to the ground, where they are collected by other workers; or the ants will truck their burden down the trunk and off to their underground nest in ceaseless columns that march day and night over well-worn trails. A colony of leaf-cutters can become enormous, its chambers and galleries reaching twenty feet below ground and containing more than half a million individuals.
(228 Jean Phillipe Varin/Jacana; 229 Harry N. Darrow)

232. *Among the larger orb weavers of the family Araneidae, the Garden Spider (Araneus diadematus) was introduced to North America from Europe and today is well established from New England to the Great Lakes as well as in the Pacific Northwest. City and suburban gardens are its haunt, and its symmetrical webs with their five- or six-sided frames are usually found spun between a house and shrubbery. The Garden Spider hangs head-down in the center of its orb, which it spins anew each night, having eaten the previous day's web. The species is sometimes called the "Cross Spider" because of a pattern on its abdomen. (Heather Angel/Biofotos)*

Spinners and Weavers

Giant orb webs, six feet across and more, hang
between treetops in Madagascar and other warm
regions as far north as Florida. The webs are the
work of calico spiders (*Nephila* spp.), orb weavers
with bodies an inch or two long and a legspan three
times as great. Such a monstrous web is held taut by
guy lines so strong that they actually pull against a
person who walks into them, a warning so firm that
there is time to back away and take another route
rather than break the line and destroy the tension on
the orb web overhead.

An orb web is the highest development of the
spider's craft. Incredibly, it is produced at night, the
spider relying on touch alone. The routine is standard
for all orb weavers (Argiopidae), and begins with a
single silken strand above where the web is to be.
Called the bridge line, this strand must be sturdy
since it is to support the whole web, the spider as she
waits in it, and whatever prey her trap may catch.
Somewhere along its length, the bridge line will be
the top strand of a generous frame, as a polygon of
silk held tightly by extra lines to bushes or heavy
objects on the ground. We may not notice the bridge
line or the frame until the spider begins to spin
radiating lines like the spokes of a wheel from the
frame to the center. The "hub" area is actually a
special little spiral of nonsticky silk upon which the
spider can rest. She leaves unconnected the radiating
lines immediately around the central spiral; these
constitute a "free zone," where she can dodge from
one side of the web to the other.

Beyond her free zone, the spider strings with truly

astonishing regularity a single spiral strand dotted with globules of nondrying adhesive. This is where insects are to be caught and held long enough for the spider to get to them. By dawn, the sticky spiral may be weighted down by dewdrops, which will later evaporate and leave the unharmed web virtually invisible. By night, the spiral will almost certainly be tattered and torn by insects, and by the spider herself as she immobilizes each insect individually and wraps it for later use. After dark, she will systematically devour her sticky strands and make a new web in the same place, sometimes with the same bridge and frame lines.

On many an orb web, such as that spun by the Black-and-yellow Garden Spider (*Argiope aurantia*), the final feature is a conspicuous zigzag strip near the spider's resting place at the center. Known as a stabilimentum, this strip was once believed to reinforce the insect trap. Young orb weavers often add several stabilimenta to their webs; older spiders add fewer. A good orb web with no stabilimenta may mean that the spider is old. Probably a stabilimentum helps a young spider to learn where an insect has blundered into the sticky spiral, giving it time to run to the victim, quiet it with venom from the tonglike fangs (chelicerae) beside the mouth, then swathe it in silk so securely that it will not be lost. Older spiders may get along without this extra guidance, having learned to feel through their feet which part of the web needs immediate attention.

A female orb weaver must be sensitive too when a male of her kind visits the boundary of her web. He has abandoned his own orb, and may spin a new one of smaller size in an outer part of hers. From this region of moderate safety he will reach out a leg and twitch her web repeatedly. If she responds as though his message were from a fly, he will rush away at once, fleeing for his life. A lack of response may indicate that she will let him approach, perhaps to mate with her. Her state of hunger may make the difference, and this he will try to discover from a distance. Her web becomes a line of communication as well as, at times, a mating-place.

Some of the orb weavers in the southeastern United States seem to have lost their ability to spin a good web. The bolas spiders (*Mastophora* spp.) stand atop some protruding branch and dangle from one front foot a silken line that ends in a sticky globule.

Sometimes they swing the globule in a circle. Eventually it may strike the body of a passing insect and let the spider haul up a meal. If the technique did not succeed so often, it would appear a most unlikely way to satisfy hunger. When we stand close to a bolas spider, with only a portion of our flashlight beam making her visible in darkness, she will continue her angling in air and swing her globule against a surprising number of moths. Turning the brightness of our lamp light on her may cause her to shut up shop, reel in her bolas, and tighten her legs about her body, as she takes on the shape of an unopened bud or a gall upon the stem—just as she does by day. Her front pair of legs require the most careful folding, for they are her longest and as well fitted as imitation fishing poles for supporting and operating the line and globule.

Indoors, neither an orb web nor a swung bolas would often reward a spider for her effort. An irregular web of sticky strands, able to hold dust particles effectively, is enough. Usually such webs are made by the cobweb weavers (Theridiidae), specifically the American House Spider (*Achaearanea tepidariorum*), a yellowish-brown creature except for its bulging abdomen, which is streaked and splotched with black and gray along its sides. The word "cobweb" comes from the Middle English *coppe*, meaning a spider. Females benefit from indoor warmth and can live as adults for more than a year, hanging in the web a series of brownish, pear-shaped cocoons full of eggs. Any egg sac that falls is carefully retrieved. An insect strong enough to escape from so loose a web is coated quickly with more silk until it can be pulled, helpless, into a secure position.

Equally irregular is the silken mesh spun by the Black Widow (*Latrodectus mactans*), a spider with a nasty reputation and equally venomous relatives over much of the world. New Zealanders know their representative by a Maori name, the *katipo*. Female Black Widows everywhere rarely leave the web, especially if it contains a tan, pear-shaped egg mass. The mother will bite aggressively at anything that comes close to the web, unless escape is particularly easy. Males do not bite. After mating, the female commonly eats the male, thus earning her popular name. Her body is seldom over half an inch long, with a nearly spherical black abdomen marked below with a red splotch shaped like an hourglass, or with two transverse red marks separated by narrow black marks. The spiderlings are orange, brown, and white; young females gain more black with each molt. A male has a rather narrower abdomen, marked with white and red along its sides. The female is more likely than the male to seek a hiding place in a vacant garment.

Most spiders, including the largest, seem reluctant to bite, and the venom of most species is no more toxic than a wasp sting when inflicted. They might make good pets and fine subjects for studying animal behavior, since they appear oblivious to confinement or unusual surroundings. Outdoors or in, a great majority lack the glands required for production of sticky threads, and must rely on other strategies to get their meals. Nonsticky silk, such as that suitable for a dragline, can still be put to effective use in many ways.

Early in the morning, when dew makes all spider webs conspicuous, is a fine time to find webspinners anywhere on Earth. Short grass strongly appeals to sheet-web weavers (Linyphiidae), which spin flat platforms and cling beneath the web until an insect settles and becomes entangled on the upper surface. This little spider (usually less than half an inch in length) pulls the insect downward through the web to inject some venom. Supposedly, the sheet protects the spider from predators. Some species construct a second sheet below the first, as though to shield themselves from dangers that might approach from ground level. Just a few build tents in which they hide, waiting until something interesting bumps into the side webbing.

Level ground or short grass attracts the funnel-web weavers (Agelenidae). These spiders spin their nonsticky sheets, then make a funnel-shaped pocket at one side in which to wait. Some of these weavers create an extra three-dimensional barrier web several inches higher than their main platform, apparently as an obstacle into which a flying insect will fall, whence it can be retrieved by the alert spider. The funnel-web weaver rushes back to its lair with its prey, remaining out of sight until it finishes its meal or another victim arrives.

The persistence of spiders as they construct their insect traps has been immortalized in fable, such as the legend that Scotsmen retell endlessly about Robert the Bruce. "If at first you don't succeed, try, and try again." Eventually the spider that Robert watched completed her web perfectly, after many a calamity. Inspired by this spider, Robert the Bruce renewed his campaign against all odds, and finally freed Scotland in 1318.

On many a field trip in various lands we become impressed by the same persistence, perhaps where a nursery-web spider (Pisauridae) has tied together strands enclosing an entire bush. Somewhere in this array of planes, oriented in many directions, the spider extrudes her eggs and wraps them securely in a silken sac. She guards them until they hatch and the spiderlings disperse. By this time, the summer may be gone, while the bush remains still shrouded in her silk.

Some of the nursery-web spiders have the almost magical ability to run over the surface of a pond or stream without even wetting their feet. We meet them on the pilings of a dock, where the spider's brown legs may spread almost three inches across. A spider's vision should be keen, with eight eyes in two rows across the front of her body. If we disturb her, she may run down to the water and scamper across the surface without sinking in. Sometimes this incredible creature earns her name of fishing spider (*Dolomedes* spp.) by climbing down a support and waiting underwater until a minnow or tadpole swims within snatching distance. She then suspends her respiration, as though holding her breath, until she emerges again into air and can ventilate the lungs which open below her abdomen a short distance ahead of her spinnerets. She has little use for silk, making no web of any kind but wrapping her eggs into spherical masses, then carrying them about, grasped by the fingerlike appendages (pedipalps) close to her mouth.

A European Fishing Spider, *Argyroneta aquatica* of the family Argyronetidae, goes to far more trouble. She spends almost her whole life underwater, and fashions between aquatic plants an airtight silken living bell. On trip after trip to the surface, she extends her abdomen and legs out of the water, then goes below again, appearing silvery with a layer of air adhering to her body hairs. She scrapes off the air under her diving bell and fills it or renews the supply where she feeds, molts, mates, and rears her young. To obtain food for her offspring and herself, she creeps among the submerged plants, catching insect larvae, mites, and other sorts of prey that ordinarily meet no spider of any kind.

On land, we can always distinguish a fishing spider from a wolf spider (Lycosidae) if they have egg sacs to carry, for a wolf spider hangs hers on behind, tight up against her spinnerets. She makes no web, but may use her silk on occasion to net some struggling prey, as well as to coat her eggs and make them easier to carry. Her hatchlings ride piggyback upon their mother as she scampers along a woodland path or across a beach, until they are old enough to disperse and fend for themselves. Her body and theirs blend harmoniously with the background, as does the fine strand of dragline each wolf spider pays out as she goes.

Daytime pursuit or ambush appeals more to the lynx spiders (Oxypodidae), which use their silk in the same limited ways as the wolf spiders. Most lynx spiders are tropical, but some are relentless hunters of prey on vegetation in the United States and Europe. The Green Lynx Spider (*Peucetia viridans*), which is found in Mexico and the southern United States, spends weeks standing guard over the egg mass she has anchored to a leaf and covered with a sheet of silk. Eventually, the spiderlings hatch out; mother and offspring then disperse, each spinning a dragline as it goes.

Come with us now to a meadow where white daisies bloom in early summer and Black-eyed Susans later in the season. These flowers offer white petals and then golden ones, which correspond to the hues of a crab spider (Thomisidae) as it ages. This color scheme lets the spider lie in ambush, wonderfully camouflaged, until some suitable insect arrives as prey. Size seems not to matter, for we have seen a big bumblebee hanging over the side of a daisy, with a crab spider clinging tight to the bee without letting go of the flower. Crab spiders hold their legs out flat to the sides, and are able to run backward, sideways or forward with equal ease. They make no snares, retreats, or overwintering webs, but provide a dragline wherever they go. The male crab spider reveals a different use for silk. He may throw a loose webbing over a prospective mate, as though to tie her down until he can mate with her. Subsequently, she is likely to provide a silken sac for her eggs and guard them for a time, or until her death leaves her hatchlings to start out as orphans.

A far greater favorite of ours is the little Zebra Spider (*Salticus scenicus*), nattily marked in black and white and common almost anywhere in the Northern Hemisphere. Each one looks back at us through an oversize pair of eyes, clearly aware that we exist but are too large for prey. Like all jumping spiders (Salticidae), it has keener vision than other arachnids and can quickly size up a situation, including the exact distance and direction in which to leap to capture a fly ten inches away. Rarely will it miss its target and require the assistance of the silken dragline it spins out as it leaps.

Male jumping spiders appear to count on the sharp eyes and alertness of prospective mates. The male approaches slowly from in front of a female he sees, and helps her recognize him by waving his front legs and the bulb-ended palps beside his mouth. His semaphore signals are in a code she understands. Will she respond to him that she is too hungry to be interested in sex and that he should go elsewhere? Or will she indicate her readiness for his approach as a suitor rather than a meal? He may continue sending his messages for five minutes before he gets an answer he can trust.

The most incredible of jumping spiders are those found at 22,000 feet on the snowy slopes of Mount Everest. Are they wind-blown juveniles that spun too long a dragline in a gale at some lower elevation, only to be torn loose and lifted so high? A British naturalist, Major R. W. G. Hingston, suggested that they arrived this way, feeding on wind-propelled insects as well as smaller spiders. Perhaps they have survived chiefly by cannibalism. Climbers on a recent expedition confirmed the existence of these jumping spiders and discovered the rest of the food web of which they are a continuing part. The spiders eat small flies and springtails, which feed in turn upon bits of fungus, rotting fragments of vegetation, and an abundance of pollen—all wind-carried from lower levels. Had the obvious spiders not been there, ready to jump over sun-warmed snowfields, the insects on which they feed and the pollen might never have been discovered. The bottom of every exposed rock face seems to be a collection center for the debris that nourishes such lofty spiders.

More power might be expected from the enormous spiders of the American Southwest—the tarantulas (Theraphosidae); South Africans know them as

Monkey Spiders, and Latin Americans call them Bird Spiders. The largest of these hairy monsters, from the Amazon basin, reach 3½ inches long, with a ten-inch legspan. Most of these blackish-brown creatures live on the ground, where they hide all day in burrows lined near the top with silk. Others climb trees in the rainforest, and there may occasionally catch a bird, lizard, or small snake. They hunt in darkness and have dispensed with using a dragline altogether. In this respect they resemble the much smaller trapdoor spiders (Ctenizidae), such as those we find on well-drained slopes near the Pacific Ocean in California. The related trapdoor spiders (Migidae) of the southern hemisphere excavate hiding places and cap them with a hinged door in the trunks of tree ferns in New Zealand or the soft bark of other trees in Australia and South Africa.

A trapdoor spider uses silk to line the whole of its sheltering tunnel, and employs an additional amount to consolidate a flat packet of earth as the trapdoor, which is hinged to the silken tube along one side. The spider holds the door tightly shut by forcing her poison fangs into the silk that covers the inner side of the trapdoor and suspending herself from it. She will brace her legs to hold her door shut if anyone tries to pry it open, and can exert a force of fourteen ounces —140 times her own weight. She will not let go until the door gapes a fraction of an inch. Then she admits defeat by plunging to safety at the bottom of her hideaway.

Under normal circumstances, a trapdoor spider waits just inside the door, alert to the slightest vibrations within her surroundings, even if no more vigorous than that caused by the footsteps of an insect walking past. Excited by the footsteps, the spider raises her door a little, then darts out at the critical moment and returns backward at top speed to haul her prey into her lair. The job is done in a fraction of a second —a mere blink of a human eye. Her magic is not sleight-of-hand but something quicker, a vanishing act that has been performed for many millions of years—in fact almost as long as there have been insects for her to catch.

241. *On a September morning in northern Michigan, the complex web of a Bowl-and-Doily Spider* (Frontinella pyramitela) *is easy to discover amid the blueberry leaves. Found across North America, this tiny spider, a mere eighth of an inch long, spins two separate webs in its ten-inch-wide snare. One is shaped like a shallow bowl, the second like a horizontal sheet, or doily. The spider hangs below the bowl and if an insect becomes entangled, it pulls the prey through the sheet and wraps it up. The lower sheet is believed to provide protection against predators attacking from below.* (John Shaw)

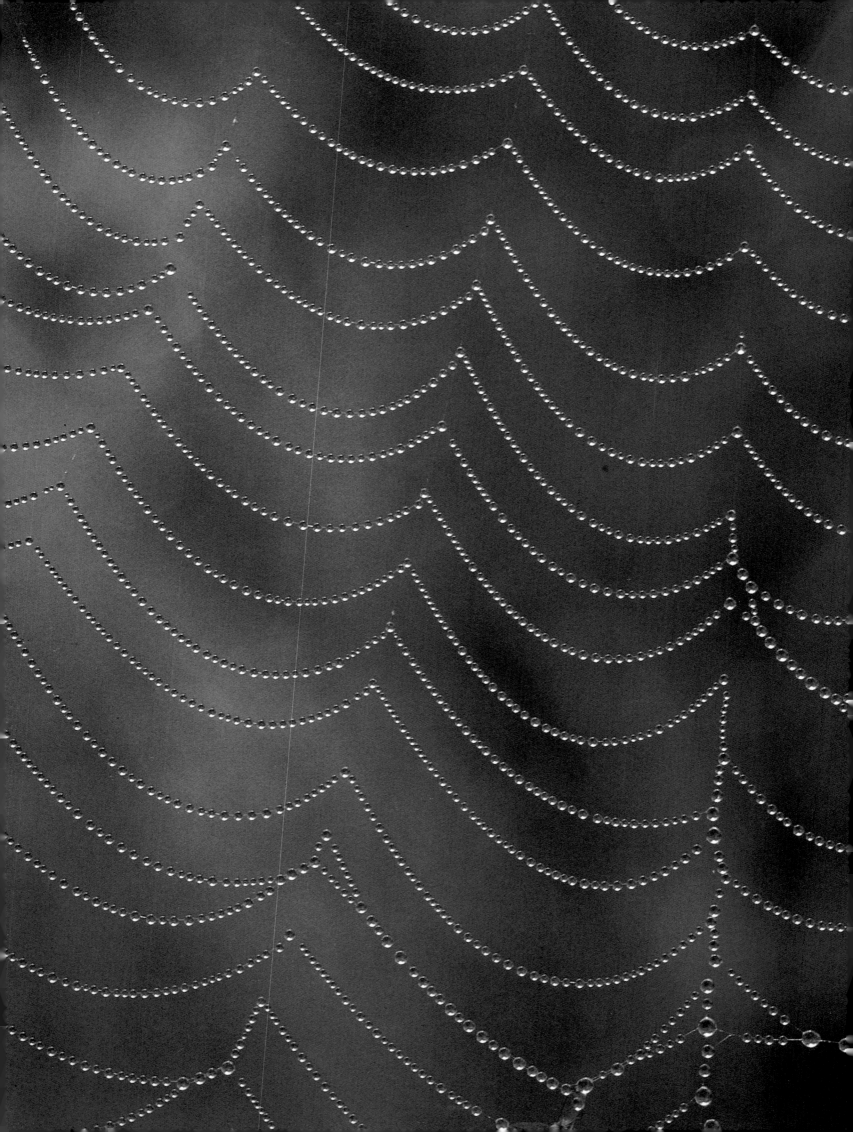

242. *Working in complete darkness, orb weavers* (Araneus spp.) *create a new web each night by touch alone. Although no human can equal this engineering feat, we can marvel at the results by going afield at dawn when the webs are sparkling with dew. Worldwide there are about 2,500 species of orb weavers, each of which has a characteristic web pattern.* (John Shaw)

243. *The Golden-silk Spider* (Nephila clavipes) *of dark woods and swamps in Florida belongs to a genus of tropical and subtropical spiders noted for their great round webs of golden silk. The female Golden-silk Spider has a body an inch long; males are only one-eighth her size. Tropical members of the genus are larger, and hang webs several feet in diameter across forest paths and high in the trees. The strands are so strong they can ensnare hummingbirds and bats; indeed, South Sea islanders use the webs as bags and fish nets.* (Lynn M. Stone)

246 *overleaf. Crab spiders have good vision for movement, and rely on strategy for their livelihood. This representative from Panama, a member of the genus* Epicadus, *mimics a bird dropping, on which some insects feed. The spider can be found sitting on either flowers or leaves, waiting for prey to blunder within reach.* (Edward S. Ross)

244. *Orchard spiders* (Leucauge spp.) *are common in shrubby meadows and woodland edges from New England to Florida and westward to the prairies. Unlike orb weavers, orchard spiders spin a horizontal rather than a vertical web. The orchard spider may hang below its snare, or wait on a nearby stem with one leg in contact with a strand until the web vibrates from the struggles of a hapless victim.* (Edward S. Ross)

245. *Poised on the rays of a black-eyed Susan, a Goldenrod Spider* (Misumena vatia) *can change its color from white to yellow to blend in with the backdrop of field and garden flowers. This species is in the crab spider family* (Thomisidae), *so named because its members hold the legs to the sides in crablike fashion and can move forward, sideways, or backward. Crab spiders do not spin webs; rather they launch an ambush from flowers, seizing flies, bees, butterflies, and moths, injecting a potent poison, and sucking their victims dry. Male crab spiders often tie down prospective mates with silken strands.* (Rod Planck)

248. *A crown of hard, sharp spines identifies the Crablike Spiny Orb Weaver (Gasteracantha ellipsoides), found from North Carolina to Florida and west to California. This spider builds a vertical orb web with few or no spiral strands near the center. The female produces an egg mass late in the year, then dies. The spiderlings that hatch disperse and overwinter, and begin weaving their own webs in the spring. This spider was photographed in a mangrove on the coast of Baja California. (C. Allan Morgan)*

249 *top. One of the giant crab spiders of the family Sparassidae, a huntsman spider (Olios sp.) hangs by its silk dropline from a tree in New Guinea. Mostly tropical in distribution, huntsman spiders have legs that span as much as four inches. They are welcome residents in countless households, for they make no dust-catching webs and control offensive pests, such as cockroaches. These spiders hide in corners or crevices by day, and emerge at night to prowl. (T. W. Davies)*

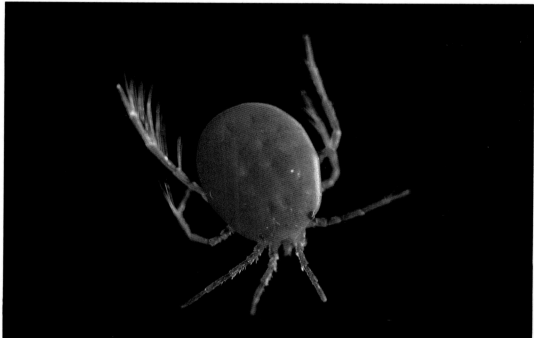

249 *bottom. No larger than a pinhead, the Red Freshwater Mite (Limnochares americana) is found in ponds and slow-moving streams across North America. Creeping on submerged vegetation or gliding through the water, it preys on small aquatic insects and mollusks. The parasitic larvae often attach themselves to nymphs of dragonflies and damselflies, becoming airborne on the newly molted adults and dropping off when the host lays its eggs. (John Shaw)*

250 *overleaf. A jumping spider (Maevia vittata) with its prey. The 2,800 species of jumping spiders in the family Salticidae have the sharpest vision of all spiders; some are able to recognize prey eight inches away. Powered by the fourth pair of legs, these small to medium-sized spiders leap on their victims, but also spin a silk dragline in case they miss the target. (Larry West)*

252. *Windscorpions (order Solpugida) are hairy, desert-dwelling animals with enormous, pincerlike jaws, called chelicerae, that work independently of each other: one pair holds the prey as the other cuts it up. Voracious nocturnal hunters, windscorpions are capable of killing small vertebrate animals, including lizards. Most windscorpions are brownish or yellowish. matching their arid habitat; the name "windscorpion" comes from the remarkable speed with which these solitary creatures dash to and from their burrows. Like this specimen from Texas, most North American windscorpions belong to the family Eremobatidae. The female hides fifty or so eggs in the soil and guards them for several weeks until they hatch.* (Robert W. Mitchell)

253 *top. With rakelike rows of spines on each jaw, or chelicera, trapdoor spiders of the family Ctenizidae dig their burrows. These cylindrical tubes are lined with silk and sealed with a silk lid, or trapdoor, which may be disguised with debris. The spider pulls the lid shut with its fangs and waits until a victim wanders by. Trapdoor spiders are largely tropical in distribution. Cyclocosmia trapdoor spiders are unusual; a member of the genus, if disturbed, runs head-first into its narrowing burrow until the tube is tightly plugged by the armor-plated, squared-off end of the spider's abdomen. In this position, holding on with its claws, the spider is nearly impossible to remove.* (Robert W. Mitchell)

253 *bottom. This burrowing wolf spider, Geolycosa pikei, lives in sand dunes and high beaches along the Great Lakes, digging a vertical burrow eight inches deep and glueing the sand particles of the walls together with silk. "Earth wolves" of this genus are found across North America, some in desert habitats, others on the dry plains; their burrows may reach as deep as three feet. Burrowing wolf spiders rarely leave their hideaways. On sunny days the female brings her large egg sac to the doorway to soak up warmth.* (Larry West)

254 *overleaf. Legends, grade-B movies, and fearsome appearance to the contrary, this desert tarantula (Aphonopelma sp.) is a docile creature and does not have a deadly bite. Indeed, the thirty or so species of tarantulas found in the southern United States are no more dangerous to humans than a wasp or bee. However, a few of the tropical tarantulas are venomous. Nocturnal creatures, tarantulas hunt by touch. Females may live twenty years; the males are killed after mating.* (C. Allan Morgan)

Notes on Photographers

Heather Angel (96, 154, 180, 232), an English professional writer and photographer, is also a qualified zoologist specializing in marine biology. She has written thirty-two books to date, including *The Natural History of Britain and Ireland*.

Heiko Bellmann (25, 114 overleaf) is an award-winning freelance photographer, as well as the author of a number of books on environmental subjects. He is a zoologist at the University of Ulm in West Germany.

René Pierre Bille (28, 212) is a Swiss naturalist, filmmaker, and photographer; his area of special interest is the wildlife of the Alps.

Søren Breiting (70 overleaf), a professional biologist, lives near Copenhagen; he is one of Denmark's leading nature photographers, and a founder of Biofoto.

Stanley Breeden (108 top left, 109 top right, 113 top left, 113 bottom, 129, 157), a native of Australia, now lives near New Delhi, India. He has photographed wildlife throughout the world and his work has been published in numerous international publications.

Sonja Bullaty and Angelo Lomeo (132) are a well-known husband-and-wife photography team. She was born in Prague, Czechoslovakia and he in New York, where they both now live and work. Their picture essays, chiefly of nature, have been widely exhibited and published.

Robert P. Carr (36, 78 overleaf, 112, 138 overleaf, 153, 190), a native of Michigan, is a regular contributor to a number of natural history magazines, including *Audubon*, *Natural History*, *National Wildlife*, and *Sierra Club*.

Robert L. Carissimi (113 top right), a resident of Waterbury, Connecticut, specializes in close-up photography. His photographs have been published in *Tropical Fish Hobbyist* and *National Wildlife* magazines.

Michel Casino (89, 173), lives in southeastern France. He specializes in the photography of insects.

Hervé Chaumeton (80, 193 top), a resident of Camalières, France, holds a master's degree in biology. For more than ten years he has travelled widely on photographic assignments for various French scientific organizations and museums.

Harry N. Darrow (34 overleaf, 141 bottom, 142 overleaf, 229), a retired bank officer, has been photographing nature for over twenty years. He specializes in birds in flight, but also enjoys taking all manner of fauna and flora.

Thomas W. Davies (37, 108 bottom left, 136 top, 137, 160, 249 top) is a lepidopterist with the California Academy of Sciences in San Francisco. He has been photographing wildlife since 1954 and has travelled extensively in the South Pacific collecting and photographing butterflies and other insects.

Edward R. Degginger (41 bottom), a retired research chemist, has been a freelance photographer for over twelve years. More than 4,000 of his pictures, spanning a wide range of subjects, have been published in books and magazines.

Cyril de Klemm (174 overleaf) is a French wildlife photographer living in Paris.

Adrian J. Dignan (158 overleaf), a former stockbroker, lives in Freeport, New York. For the last seventeen years, he has been active as a freelance nature photographer. Birds are his favorite subject, but he photographs everything that "flies, crawls, or swims."

Jack Drafahl (106 overleaf) taught photography for many years before becoming a surgical photographer for the Good Samaritan Hospital in Portland, Oregon. He is also a successful freelance nature photographer and runs Kritter Labs, a wildlife photography agency.

Harry Ellis (90 top left, 130 overleaf, 136 center), a professional nature photographer and writer for over twenty years, lives in the heart of the Blue Ridge Mountains of North Carolina. His essays and photographs have appeared in most of the major nature magazines both here and abroad.

Jeffrey Foott (222 overleaf, 224 overleaf, 230 overleaf) lives in western Wyoming near Grand Teton National Park. Trained as a marine biologist, he has photographed and filmed wildlife from Alaska to the Antarctic.

François Gohier (90 top right, 94 overleaf) is a French freelance writer and photographer who specializes in the wildlife of South America. His articles and photographs have appeared in many publications, including *The Audubon Society Encyclopedia of Animal Life.*

Jean Paul Hervy (33 bottom, 93) is an entomologist with the French Office for Overseas Scientific Research (ORSTOM). He presently lives and works in Dakar, Senegal.

Stephen J. Krasemann (60, 226), a nature photographer living in southwestern Wisconsin, has contributed his work to numerous publications, including *National Geographic, Audubon,* and *Natural History* magazines.

Charles Krebs (57, 69 bottom, 208), a native of Long Island, New York, now pursues a career as a freelance photographer in the Pacific Northwest. He also teaches workshops on nature and close-up photography.

Dwight R. Kuhn (66 overleaf, 69 top, 196) teaches biology and chemistry in Maine and has a penchant for nature photography. His published work is noted for its detailed studies of natural history subjects.

Cal and Marion Latch (56, 209 bottom) live and work near Portland, Oregon. Specialists in nature photography, they are both Star Exhibitors of the Photographic Society of America.

Patrick Lorne (72, 116, 133 top) is a French freelance photographer living near Paris.

Raymond A. Mendez (i, ii overleaf, iv overleaf, vii overleaf), a native of New York City, worked for twelve years in the Exhibition Department of the American Museum of Natural History before becoming a full-time freelance photographer. His work has been published in numerous nature magazines, including *Discover, Geo,* and *Natural History.*

Robert W. Mitchell (30 overleaf, 53, 54, 55, 77, 92, 108 bottom center, 109 bottom right, 155 bottom, 177 top, 177 bottom, 205, 252, 253 top), a professor of biology at Texas Technical University in Lubbock, has been a natural history photographer for twenty years. Widely published, he specializes both in close-up photography and the lives of cave-dwelling animals.

C. Allan Morgan (108–109 top center, 144, 248, 254 overleaf) has had his nature photographs featured in scores of books and magazines. He has spent most of the past twenty years in Colorado and Arizona. He is presently working on a book about the deserts of the Southwest.

Klaus Paysan (164) is an award-winning German wildlife photographer. He also runs a nature photography agency, Bildarchiv Paysan, based in Stuttgart.

Carroll W. Perkins (26), a resident of Edmonton, Alberta, has been involved in nature photography for twenty years. His photos have been published in numerous books and magazines.

Pierre Pilloud (29 bottom, 193 bottom), a French freelance photographer, lives near Paris. His photographic specialties include insects and botany.

Rod Planck (133 bottom, 134 overleaf, 162 overleaf, 245) is a twenty-three year old resident of Spruce, Michigan. His work has been published in several magazines, as well as in calendars and as posters.

Ivan Polunin (40, 41 top, 155 top left), a well-respected photographer of wildlife of the Pacific and the Far East, is on the Faculty of Medicine at the University of Singapore.

Betty Randall (14 overleaf, 16, 155 top right) holds an M.A. in biochemistry from the University of California, Berkeley. After twenty years of laboratory research work, she has become a professional photographer. Her work has appeared in many nature publications.

Edward S. Ross (27 top, 29 top, 44, 58 overleaf, 64, 65, 68, 117 top, 118 overleaf, 156 top, 192, 206 overleaf, 209 top, 210 overleaf, 244, 246 overleaf), Curator of Insects at the California Academy of Sciences in San Francisco, is a pioneer of insect photography. His work has appeared in hundreds of publications.

Kjell B. Sandved (27 bottom, 62 overleaf, 110 overleaf, 161 top, 161 bottom, 189), in addition to working as a nature photographer, produces films at the Museum of Natural History of the Smithsonian Institution. He also delivers lectures on animal behavior throughout the United States for the Smithsonian Associates.

John Shaw (32, 42 overleaf, 61, 105, 117 bottom, 120, 140, 221, 227, 241, 242, 249 bottom) is a professional photographer living in Richland, Michigan. His photographs have appeared in such magazines as *National Wildlife* and *Audubon* as well as in numerous books, filmstrips, and advertisements.

Lynn M. Stone (156 bottom, 243) is an English teacher in West Aurora, Illinois, as well as a freelance nature photographer and journalist. He has travelled widely throughout the country photographing wildlife.

Jean Philippe Varin (228) was born in Clermont-Ferand, France. A biologist and photographer, he founded Jacana, the well-known French nature photography agency. He is the co-author of *Photographing Wildlife*.

Michel Viard (156 center), born in Avignon, now lives and works in the south of France. He is presently preparing a book on the famous French entomologist Jean Henri Fabre.

Larry West (33 top, 38 overleaf, 91, 141 top left, 141 top right, 176, 178 overleaf, 191, 194 overleaf, 250 overleaf, 253 bottom) lives in Mason, Michigan, about one mile from his place of birth. He describes himself as a naturalist rather than a photographer; nevertheless, his pictures have been widely published in both magazines and books.

Belinda Wright (90 bottom, 136 bottom), a wildlife filmmaker and photographer, lives in India. Her work has appeared in many publications, including the *Audubon Society Book of Trees* and *National Geographic*.

Index

Numbers in italic indicate pictures